YOUR WORD SPEAKS TO ME

SCRIPTURE MEDITATIONS
FOR DAILY LIVING

GEORGE MARTIN

the WORD
among us®
press

Versions of the reflections in this book appeared in *New Covenant* magazine.
Some were collected in *Your Word* (Servant Books, 1980).

The Word Among Us Press
9639 Doctor Perry Road
Ijamsville, Maryland 21754
www.wordamongus.org

10 09 08 07 06   1 2 3 4 5

ISBN: 1-59325-068-1

Unless otherwise noted, Scripture passages contained herein are from the New
Revised Standard Version Bible: Catholic Edition, copyright © 1989, 1993 Division of Christian Education of the National Council of the Churches of Christ in
the United States. All rights reserved. Used with permission.

Cover design by Evelyn Harris

Made and printed in the United States of America

Library of Congress Cataloging-in-Publication Data

Martin, George, 1939-
Your word speaks to me : scripture meditations for daily living / by
George Martin.
    p. cm.
Includes index.
ISBN 1-59325-068-1 (alk. paper)
1. Bible--Meditations. I. Title.
BS483.5.M365 2006
242'.5--dc22
                            2005031022

Table of Contents

INTRODUCTION

Sometimes simple decisions have far-reaching conse-quences. This book has its roots in two decisions I made four decades ago.

In 1964 I decided to read the Bible every day during Lent. I had never read Scripture before—I didn't even own a Bible—but I thought that reading Scripture was a good Lenten resolu-tion. I bought a New Testament and I discovered God's word that Lent. When Lent was over, I kept on reading, praying each day, "Lord, speak to me through your words in Scrip-ture." Scripture came alive for me.

Beginning in 1968 I helped make practical arrangements for a monthly "Day of Renewal" for those involved in the Catholic charismatic renewal in Michigan. I reserved a church hall where we could meet and mailed out a monthly notice with a map showing how to get there. After we settled on a regular meeting place, the map became unnecessary, and I decided to replace it with a short reflection on Scripture—no sense wasting the space! The words of Scripture had great meaning for me, and I wanted to share the riches I found in them with others.

The statewide "Day of Renewal" was discontinued in favor of regional meetings in 1970, which was also the year that a "pastoral newsletter" began publication in Ann Arbor. I was invited to continue my Scripture meditations in its pages. The editor used a verse from Psalm 119 as the heading for my reflections: "Your word is a lamp to my feet and a light to my path" (Psalm 119:105). In 1971, the pastoral news-letter was revamped and became *New Covenant* magazine; my "Your Word" Scripture meditations, as my column was called, appeared in it until *New Covenant* ceased publication in 2002.

I decided to read Scripture daily during Lent; then I decided to write about Scripture as a space-filler in a meeting notice. Not earthshaking decisions, but they led to my writing hundreds of Scripture reflections over the next four decades.

Some of the early meditations were collected and published as pamphlets by Dove Publications of Pecos, New Mexico. In 1980 Servant Books brought out a collection of reflections written in the late 1970s as a book titled *Your Word*, now out of print. This present book, *Your Word Speaks to Me*, includes some meditations that appeared in the 1980 book along with others that appeared in *New Covenant* magazine in the early 1980s. Among them are some of my all-time favorites.

That is the skeleton of the story of this book but not its flesh. The flesh is my approach to Scripture and what I hope readers will get out of my Scripture reflections.

Here too I must go back four decades. Around the same time I began to read the Bible, I came across two writings that had—and have—a great influence on how I read Scripture. One was a pamphlet, now out of print, "Learning to Read the Bible" by Pius Parsch (Liturgical Press, 1963; a condensed version appeared in the November 1963 issue of *The Bible Today*). Parsch advocated reading Scripture as God's communication to us: "God is our father. The Scriptures are his letter, a father's letter to his children. . . . When we begin to read the Bible we should say to God: 'Speak, Father, for your child is listening.'"

I found a similar approach to Scripture in the writings of Søren Kierkegaard, a nineteenth-century Danish Lutheran. In his book *For Self-Examination*, he compared Scripture to a love letter that demanded personal, not detached, reading. He advised that as you read Scripture, "remember to say to yourself incessantly: 'It is talking to me; I am the one it is speaking about.'"

We need to study Scripture in order to understand it. We should not identify the inspired meaning of Scripture with the first thing that pops into our minds when we read a passage. According to the Second Vatican Council, "In order to see clearly what God wanted to communicate to us" through Scripture, we "should carefully investigate what meaning the sacred writers really intended, and what God wanted to manifest by means of their words" (*On Divine Revelation*, 12). For example, Paul intended to communicate certain things to the Christians of Corinth when he wrote to them. He told them, "We write you nothing other than what you can read and also understand" (2 Corinthians 1:13). Because Paul wrote under the inspiration of the Holy Spirit, what he intended to convey was God's message to the Corinthians. To understand God's message, the Corinthians had to understand the meaning of Paul's words. We also need to understand what the inspired authors convey by their words in order to understand the message of Scripture for us.

At the same time, we also need to take what we read in Scripture as God's personal communication to us. We must, for example, place ourselves among the "you" John addresses when he states that he wrote "so that *you* may come to believe that Jesus is the Messiah, the Son of God, and that through believing *you* may have life in his name" (John 20:31). I tried to present how to go about reading Scripture with both understanding and personal application in my 1975 book, *Reading Scripture as the Word of God* (available in its fourth edition from Servant Books/St. Anthony Messenger Press).

My aim in writing Scripture meditations is to probe the meaning of a verse or passage or theme of Scripture and draw out implications and applications for us as Christians today. My best meditations spring from an insight: "Oh—*that's* what these words mean; I never grasped it before." My best meditations are a bridge between what Scripture meant when it was written and what Scripture means for us in our Christian lives today.

My hope is that my reflections will prove to be useful bridges for you, as you ponder the words of Scripture as God's word to you. Who knows what the results might be!

George Martin
March 1, 2006

PART ONE

JESUS, OUR SAVIOR

I. WHAT'S IN A NAME?

> Now the birth of Jesus the Messiah took place in this way. When his mother Mary had been engaged to Joseph, but before they lived together, she was found to be with child from the Holy Spirit. Her husband Joseph, being a righteous man and unwilling to expose her to public disgrace, planned to dismiss her quietly. But just when he had resolved to do this, an angel of the Lord appeared to him in a dream and said, "Joseph, son of David, do not be afraid to take Mary as your wife, for the child conceived in her is from the Holy Spirit. She will bear a son, and you are to name him Jesus, for he will save his people from their sins."
>
> When Joseph awoke from sleep, he did as the angel of the Lord commanded him; he took her as his wife, but had no marital relations with her until she had borne a son; and he named him Jesus.
>
> —Matthew 1:18-21, 24-25

In the Bible, a person's name was not an arbitrary identification tag, but an expression of the nature and character of that person. A person's name revealed his or her identity, and hence in some sense one's name *was* one's identity. When God intervened in people's lives, he sometimes changed their names to signify the change he was working in them. Thus Abram became Abraham (Genesis 17:5) and Jacob became Israel (32:28).

It is significant, therefore, that the angel instructed Joseph what to name the son that Mary would bear. God didn't choose the name Jesus simply because he liked the name, but because it would reveal something important about his Son.

Like many Hebrew and Aramaic names, the name Jesus meant something, just as the English name Smith originally signified a blacksmith and the name Johnson once meant the son of John. The name given to the son of Mary was Yeshua in Aramaic—a shortened version of an older Hebrew compound name—which came into English as the name Jesus. Jesus was not the first one to bear this name. The first instance we have in Scripture was a man originally named Hoshea, who was given the new name Yehoshua by Moses (Numbers 13:16)—the man we know as Joshua, the successor of Moses. In Hebrew the name Yehoshua/Joshua means "Yahweh [God's personal name in the Old Testament] saves" or "Yahweh is salvation," and this was the name, in its later form, that the angel decreed should be given to Mary's child.

In the first century, Jesus (or Yeshua) was a very popular name among Jews; Joshua had been a great Israelite leader, and many boys were named in memory of him. The significance of Jesus' name, therefore, doesn't lie in its uniqueness but in its meaning, "Yahweh saves."

Note the angel's words to Joseph, "You are to name him Jesus, for *he* will save his people from their sins" (Matthew 1:21). We might have expected the angel to say, "You are to name him Jesus because God will save his people." No: he is to be named "Yahweh saves" because he—Jesus—is the one who is going to save his people. The angel's words reveal that the son of Mary was to be unlike any other child who bore the name Jesus, for *this* Jesus would be the one through whom God would bring salvation to his people. All others who bore the name Jesus would testify by their name to the fact that God saves; this Jesus would not only testify to that fact but would bring it about. This Jesus would *be* the salvation of God that his name proclaimed.

When Peter and John were brought before the Sanhedrin for healing someone who was sick, Peter boldly stated, "This man is standing before you in good health by the name of Jesus Christ of Nazareth. . . . There is salvation in no one else, for there is no other name under heaven given among mortals by which we must be saved" (Acts 4:10, 12).

We are given salvation in the name of Jesus because the name of Jesus expresses who he is and what he has done for us. In Jesus, God saves us; Jesus is the salvation of God come among us. It is Jesus, the Son of God born of Mary, who saves us from our sins, in fulfillment of the name that God chose for him. Jesus was not only *named* "Yahweh is our salvation"; he *is* the salvation of God for us.

2. GOD'S DESIGN

> [Jesus] came to his hometown and began to teach the people in their synagogue, so that they were astounded and said, "Where did this man get this wisdom and these deeds of power? Is not this the carpenter's son? Is not his mother called Mary? And are not his brothers James and Joseph and Simon and Judas? And are not all his sisters with us? Where then did this man get all this?" And they took offense at him. But Jesus said to them, "Prophets are not without honor except in their own country and in their own house." And he did not do many deeds of power there, because of their unbelief.
> —Matthew 13:54-58

It would have been easier for the people of Nazareth to accept Jesus as the Messiah if he had been borne into their midst on a fiery chariot, descending from the clouds with an escort of angels. But he was not. He was born on earth through Mary; he was "the carpenter's son." In his appearance he was like any other man.

There is a human thirst for the spectacular, for the manifestly supernatural, for signs and wonders. They were present in the life of Jesus, but not as much as some would have liked. At the beginning of his ministry, Jesus refused Satan's temptations to turn rock into bread or jump down from the pinnacle of the temple (Matthew 4:3-7), although both would have been displays of divine power. Jesus refused to provide signs from heaven for those who demanded them (Mark 8:11-12). And at the end of his ministry he refrained from calling down twelve legions of angels to protect him from arrest (Matthew 26:53). Nor did he heed the cries of the crowd, "If you are the Son of God, come down from the cross. . . . Let him come down from the cross now, and we will believe in him" (27:40, 42).

When Jesus sat down to eat at the same table with sinners, religious leaders were shocked (Mark 2:15-16). When he performed the lowly service of washing feet, his disciples were embarrassed and confused (John 13:3-8). When he accepted death as his Father's will for him, his followers were scandalized and scattered (Mark 14:50).

If we had our way, we would remake Jesus into someone more to our liking—someone whose triumph over evil was more obviously complete, someone who would not invite us to suffer in imitation of him. If we had our way, we would redesign Christianity so that signs and wonders abounded and faith came effortlessly, so that our cross was comfortable and our life an unending series of triumphs.

But Jesus is the design of the Father for us and the norm for what it means to be Christian. In his life we find the pattern that we are called to imitate. It is a pattern made up of humble service and of laying down one's very life. God offers us eternal life if we follow in the footsteps of Jesus; God's design is that we conform ourselves to his Son, both in dying and in rising.

3. LIKE US IN EVERY WAY

[Jesus] had to become like his brothers and sisters in every respect, so that he might be a merciful and faithful high priest in the service of God, to make a sacrifice of atonement for the sins of the people. Because he himself was tested by what he suffered, he is able to help those who are being tested.

For we do not have a high priest who is unable to sympathize with our weaknesses, but we have one who in every respect has been tested as we are, yet without sin. Let us therefore approach the throne of grace with boldness, so that we may receive mercy and find grace to help in time of need.

—Hebrews 2:17-18; 4:15-16

The letter to the Hebrews teaches that Jesus was like us "in every respect" and was tested ("tempted" in some translations) "in every respect" that we are, although without ever sinning. We find it easy enough to believe that Jesus never sinned; however, it is a little harder for us to accept the fact that Jesus was tempted in every way that we are and was like us (aside from sin) in every way.

Jesus is the Son of God. Surely, we think, he must have been immune to many of the temptations that plague us—temptations to laziness, irritability, jealousy, and giving up. Surely his being the Son of God must have meant that even in his human nature he was above the weaknesses that afflict us. He could have been like us, but only like us in our better moments, when we feel pure and selfless and close to God.

Yet the Letter to the Hebrews says that Jesus is like us in *every* respect. If the inspired author had wanted to say that Jesus was like us only when we were being as perfect as God's grace and our own willpower could make us, he could have said that. But he didn't. He said that Jesus was like us in every respect except for sinning. That covers a lot of ground.

We may find it hard to imagine that Jesus had the same temptations we have. We may believe that he was tempted, but only as befitted the Son of God: he was tempted to turn stones into bread, to float down from the pinnacle of the temple. Our temptations are of a seemingly different order: we are tempted to anger and irritability, to dishonesty and lying, to selfishness and impurity, even to despair. Yet Jesus' temptations weren't limited to his use of power. The Letter to the Hebrews teaches that Jesus was tested or tempted in all of the same ways we are.

The author of Hebrews draws an important lesson from Jesus' similarity to us. Because Jesus was like us in every way, he is able to sympathize with us and be merciful to us when we fail. He has compassion for us in our condition, because he assumed our condition and experienced what we experience. His is the sympathy of one who has gone through what we go through.

Jesus didn't live his life immune to pain and disappointment and trial. Therefore he truly understands us and everything we go through. Hence he invites us to turn to him in our need and distress, in our weakness and temptation.

We sometimes have a hard time turning to Jesus, however, precisely when we most need his help. If we are feeling close to God, it is easy to turn to Jesus in prayer. But when we are feeling mediocre and unworthy, distracted and tempted, then we sometimes hold back. We may even want to hide our condition from Jesus, lest we have to admit how attracted we are by the temptations afflicting us and how weak we are in resisting them. We may only want to enter into the presence of Jesus when we feel more worthy to do so.

YOUR WORD SPEAKS TO ME

The author of Hebrews understood our reluctance to come to Jesus when we are most in need of his saving grace; that is why he wrote what he wrote. He urges us to "approach the throne of grace with boldness" so that we may find "help in time of need" (4:16). He reassures us that Jesus understands us and is willing to embrace us in the condition we are in, just as Jesus willingly and fully embraced the human condition himself. He emphasizes that Jesus is merciful precisely because he was like us in every way and knows how great our need for mercy is. He exhorts us to come in our need and weakness and temptation to him who was like us in every way and yet, as the Son of God, is able to save us.

4. BELIEVING WITHOUT SEEING

Then he said to Thomas, "Put your finger here and see my hands. Reach out your hand and put it in my side. Do not doubt but believe." Thomas answered him, "My Lord and my God!" Jesus said to him, "Have you believed because you have seen me? Blessed are those who have not seen and yet have come to believe."

Now Jesus did many other signs in the presence of his disciples, which are not written in this book. But these are written so that you may come to believe that Jesus is the Messiah, the Son of God, and that through believing you may have life in his name.

—John 20:27-31

John's gospel was the last to be written; it probably received its final editing around the end of the first century. John wrote for those who had not known Jesus during his life on earth but had received the message of salvation through the preaching of the early church.

The incident of Thomas's doubting that Jesus was truly risen and alive therefore had special meaning for those who first read John's gospel. They had not seen Jesus during the years he walked the paths of Galilee; they had not heard him teach in the temple; they had not witnessed his resurrection. Yet because of the preaching of the church, they had come to believe that Jesus was truly risen and the Son of God. This incident in John's gospel commended the faith of those who had not seen Jesus after his resurrection and yet still believed in him.

John's gospel is written equally for us. It makes no difference whether we are one generation or one hundred generations removed from the day when Jesus rose from the dead; we are basically in the same situation as those for whom John wrote. He wrote so that we too might believe that Jesus is the Christ and the Son of God, and so that we too might receive life from him.

We may once have had a vivid awareness of the presence of the risen Jesus in our lives, but this awareness may have gradually dimmed. Most of our waking hours are taken up by the many tasks we have to do. We know that we can go for stretches of time without even thinking of Jesus. It is not that we want to ignore him; it's just that the insistence of children clamoring to be fed, or customers waiting to be served, or bills needing to be paid often takes our attention away from Jesus.

Life was probably no less distracting in the Roman Empire. John certainly did not write for those living in a culture that was more Christian than our own. Nor has the nature of being a follower of Jesus changed in the last nineteen-hundred years. Jesus was not present to the Christians living toward the end of the first century in any way that he is not present to us. We can therefore take the account of Thomas's doubting and coming to believe as having been written for us today and carrying a message of encouragement for us.

Our faith is not in any way defective because we do not physically see Jesus. Faith is precisely in the unseen. The Letter to the Hebrews terms it "the conviction of things not seen" (Hebrews 11:1); Paul states that "we walk by faith, not by sight" (2 Corinthians 5:7).

Jesus said that those who do not see him physically yet believe are blessed. Jesus loves those who persevere in their faith in him despite the unbelief around them and the distractions of their lives. They are the ones who have found life in the name of Jesus, who have welcomed the message of the gospel and confessed to Jesus, "My Lord and my God!"—without ever having had to see him.

5. FRIEND AND SAVIOR

Jesus loved Martha and her sister and Lazarus.
—John 11:5

Martha and Mary and their brother, Lazarus, lived in Bethany, a small town about two miles from Jerusalem. The gospels tell us that they were Jesus' friends; there is no indication, however, that he called them to follow him as traveling disciples. Rather, the gospels portray their house as a place where Jesus would stop during his travels, a place where he could get a meal, a place where he could rest and spend the night.

Martha is portrayed as the one busy cooking and serving (Luke 10:40; John 12:2), Mary, as the one who sits at Jesus' feet (Luke 10:39; John 12:3). Jesus calls Lazarus his "friend" (John 11:11). The gospels record no words of Lazarus and only tell us that Lazarus ate with Jesus (12:2) and came forth from the tomb at Jesus' command (11:43-44).

What was the relationship like between Jesus and the members of the Bethany household? The gospel tells us that Martha and Mary and Lazarus recognized Jesus as the Christ, the Son of God (John 11:27), and knew that he had power over sickness and death. But the relationship between Martha and Mary and Lazarus and Jesus was not simply one of acknowledging him as the Messiah or revering him as a great teacher. Martha, Mary, Lazarus, and Jesus were first of all friends. They liked one another and enjoyed being with each other. They shared meals together as an expression of their friendship. As John tells us in his gospel, "Jesus loved Martha and her sister and Lazarus" (11:5).

To get an insight into this loving friendship, we can reflect on our own experiences of friendship and love. Who are our best friends? What kind of affection do we feel toward them? What kinds of things do we enjoy doing with them? What contentment do we experience in simply being with someone we love? When we are reunited with a dear friend after a long separation, what emotions of joy and gladness go through us? In times of great happiness, we wish that our most intimate friends could be with us to share the joy. And in times of sorrow, we treasure the support that comes from our closest friends, from those we know we can depend on no matter what.

Such was the relationship between Jesus and Martha, Mary, and Lazarus. They acknowledged him as Lord, but they also considered him their friend. They welcomed him to their table. They were unabashed in exhibiting their sorrow in front of him (John 11:33); their friendship was even intimate enough to involve him in their family quarrels (Luke 10:40).

Our friendship with Jesus should have the same human qualities. Even though we worship him as the Son of God, we should still strive for the same joy and affection that we have with our dearest friend, the same intimacy and sharing that

21

we have with our husband or wife. This doesn't mean that we should reduce Jesus to the level of a "good buddy"; rather, it means that he welcomes our heartfelt love as well as our worship—and that he loves us in return.

Jesus has the same love for us that he had toward Martha and Mary and Lazarus. If we know that our best friend loves us and enjoys being with us, we should know that Jesus loves us even more. Jesus wants to be present at our table. He wants to share our joys and ease our sorrows. He wants us to invite him into our lives, just as he welcomed the invitations of Martha and Mary. He wants to be present in our lives as our Lord and redeemer—but also as our friend. "I do not call you servants any longer; . . . I have called you friends" (John 15:15).

6. WHAT IS GOD LIKE?

Long ago, God spoke to our ancestors in many and various ways by the prophets, but in these last days he has spoken to us by a Son, whom he appointed heir of all things, through whom he also created the worlds. He is the reflection of God's glory and the exact imprint of God's very being, and he sustains all things by his powerful word.
—Hebrews 1:1-3

Some people are not sure whether God exists or not. Some have difficulty reconciling the presence of evil in the world with an all-powerful and loving God; others conclude from an apparent absence of God from the world that there is no God. Still others, distracted by living for the moment, don't bother themselves much about the question of God's existence.

Then there are those who believe that God exists but are unsure what God is really like. They reason that there must be some ultimate source of the universe and of life. They instinctively know that they are not simply part of some cosmic accident, without cause or purpose. But beyond believing that some being is responsible for the universe, they are unsure just what or who that being might be. Even among those who believe in God, some are much more firm in their faith in the existence of God than they are in their knowledge of what God is like.

If we had to take the path of philosophy to arrive at our knowledge of God, the way would be difficult and the results limited. But fortunately God has taken the initiative to reveal himself to us. "God spoke to our ancestors in many and various ways by the prophets" (Hebrews 1:1). God spoke to Abraham and Moses; he spoke to Isaiah and Jeremiah. The record of this revelation is contained in the Old Testament. Through its pages we can get a glimpse of who God is and what he is like. Through the record of his words and his intervention in the life of his people, we can learn much about God.

Even more fortunately for us, God was not content to allow the partial and varied revelation of the old covenant to be his last word. He spoke again, and spoke the definitive word about himself: "In these last days he has spoken to us by a Son" (Hebrews 1:2). This Son, through whom the universe came into being, "is the reflection of God's glory and the exact imprint of God's very being" (1:3). Jesus Christ, the Word made flesh, is the answer to the question of what God is like.

Jesus told his followers, "Whoever has seen me has seen the Father" (John 14:9). But what did men and women see when they gazed upon Jesus? Some saw a carpenter from Nazareth, for he was certainly that. But that was all they were able to see (Mark 6:3). Without the insight of faith, Jesus could appear to be just another craftsman from a small village.

What did those who saw Jesus through the eyes of faith see in him? What did his life tell them about God? Jesus "went about doing good and healing all who were oppressed by the devil" (Acts 10:38). He condemned sin but offered forgiveness to the sinner. He didn't turn away anyone who came to him, even if they were scruffy and sinful. He told his followers that he was in their midst to serve them (Luke 22:27), and serve them he did. He offered his life as a ransom (Mark 10:45) and voluntarily accepted a painful and ignominious death.

If the life of Jesus is a reflection of his Father, then God must likewise be concerned for his people, eager to care for them and heal them. If the example of Jesus teaches us about his Father, then God must likewise be willing to forgive and must always be ready to welcome those who turn to him. If he through whom the universe was created came in our midst to serve us, then God's love for us must truly be limitless! If he who sustains all things in existence accepted death on a cross for us, then God must indeed be very intent on redeeming us and drawing us to himself.

We could never arrive at such knowledge about God by reason alone or even by reflecting on the Old Testament. For God to reveal the full truth about himself, he had to send his Son to live among us. Now if we want to learn about God, we must gaze upon his Son.

7. AWAITING OUR INVITATION

As they came near the village to which they were going, he walked ahead as if he were going on. But they urged him strongly, saying, "Stay with us, because it is almost evening and the day is now nearly over." So he went in to stay with them. When he was at the table with them, he took bread, blessed and broke it, and gave it to them. Then their eyes were opened and they recognized him; and he vanished from their sight.

—Luke 24:28-31

The scene is a familiar one. After the crucifixion of Jesus, two of his disciples are walking on the road to Emmaus. They are downcast and dejected; their hopes for the liberation of Israel have been shattered by Jesus' death. True, some of their friends visited his tomb and found it empty, and some women claimed to have seen angels who declared that Jesus was alive. But these two disciples do not know what to make of those baffling events.

Then Jesus comes and walks by their side without their recognizing him. Jesus explains to them how he is the fulfillment of the promises of the prophets; he explains to them the meaning of their Scriptures, the books we read as the Old Testament. As he teaches them, their hearts are touched by God's presence and love.

When they arrive at their destination, they invite Jesus to stay with them. Jesus accepts their invitation and shares a meal with them. Suddenly they recognize him "in the breaking of the bread" (Luke 24:35), and they return to Jerusalem to report what has happened.

It is easy to see ourselves in these two disciples. We often have difficulty understanding the books and prophecies of the Old Testament and need someone to explain them to us, just as the disciples needed Jesus' explanation. We sometimes have a very definite but erroneous idea of what God's plans are and become dejected when they do not come to pass. When difficult times come, we become downcast and depressed. Even the encouragement and witness of friends can fail to cut through our confusion.

But most of all, we fail to recognize Jesus walking by our side. Jesus can be as near to us as he was to the two disciples on the road to Emmaus, and we can be just as unaware of his presence. Perhaps at one point in our lives he seemed close to us, just as he might have to the two disciples as they sat at his feet when he taught. But now Jesus seems absent, and we are less sure of our faith.

The two disciples recognized Jesus in "the breaking of the bread." When Luke uses this phrase in his gospel and in Acts, he is alluding to the Eucharist. It is important to note that Jesus sat down at table with the two disciples because they invited him to do so: "He walked ahead as if he were going on. But they urged him strongly, saying, 'Stay with us'" (Luke 24:28-29). They invited Jesus to lodge with them for the night and share their evening meal, and they consequently came to recognize his presence.

In the letter to the church at Laodicea in the Book of Revelation, Christ says, "Listen! I am standing at the door, knocking; if you hear my voice and open the door, I will come in to you and eat with you, and you with me" (3:20). This verse is often used by evangelists to present the need for accepting Jesus as Lord and inviting him into our lives as our Savior.

But these words were originally addressed to Christians, to those who already believed in Jesus Christ. They are an invitation for Christians to receive Jesus into their lives in a more intimate way. They are a promise that Jesus will be with those who invite him to be with them, just as he was present to the disciples on the road to Emmaus and sat down with them at table.

Jesus already walks by our side, but we may not recognize him. He has conquered death, but our faith may be too weak to perceive the implications of his victory for us. The Father's plan of salvation has been revealed to us, but we need the inspiration of the Spirit to grasp it. Jesus awaits our invitation to enter more intimately into our lives and to open our eyes to his presence.

QUESTIONS FOR REFLECTION

1. How does an understanding of Jesus' name help you to know him in a deeper way? What does praying "in the name of Jesus" mean to you?

2. How often do you find yourself struggling with expectations and desires that do not seem to fit the life of a disciple of Christ—perhaps for a more comfortable lifestyle or one without trials and crosses? What could help you to resist this temptation?

3. Do you think of Jesus as your friend? When you speak to him in prayer, how do you normally address him: as Jesus? as Lord? as Savior? as _____? What does this reveal about your relationship with him?

4. What does the Word becoming flesh and living among us tell you about God? What event in Jesus' life gives you the greatest insight into what God is like? What teaching of Jesus conveys the most to you about his Father?

5. How are you most aware of the presence of Jesus in your life? If there are times when Jesus seems absent from you, how do you react to his absence? What might you do to become more aware of his presence?

PART TWO

HEARING GOD'S WORD

1. IT'S GOOD NEWS

> The beginning of the good news of Jesus Christ, the Son of God.
> —Mark 1:1

The word "gospel" means "good news." It is important to realize that the gospel is good news—that the message of Jesus Christ is a message that is truly good news for us.

We can all too easily fall into thinking of the gospel as "mixed news"—a message that has its good points and its bad points, its advantages and its drawbacks. We can welcome those aspects of the gospel that bring joy and consolation to us, yet harbor deep-seated resentments about other aspects that make demands on our lives. We can rejoice that Jesus came to live in our midst, but resist any suggestion that we are to live in imitation of him.

For some, the gospel can even become "bad news," a series of impossible demands, a standard of conduct that we cannot measure up to, a heavy burden that we have to endure. If we allow our own faults and trials to preoccupy us, then the gospel can loom as a standard that we cannot meet. Our focus becomes limited to our unworthiness—an unworthiness that we imagine must incur God's extreme displeasure—and we lose sight of the true message of the gospel.

We need to remind ourselves that the "good news of Jesus Christ" is just that—*good* news. It is good news because it focuses on God's love, not on our sinfulness. The good news is that God loves me—and loves me despite my sinful state. The good news is that through Jesus Christ I have been given redemption. The good news is that through the presence of the Holy Spirit in me, God accepts me as his daughter or son.

If our eyes are constantly riveted on our own faults, such truths can be hard to accept. If we cannot see much that is lovable in ourselves, we imagine that God cannot either. His eyesight is better than ours, however. And even if God did agree with our assessment of ourselves, it wouldn't keep him from loving us. The *really* good news is that God loves us anyway, and is willing to go to unimaginable lengths to rescue us from our sinfulness. "God proves his love for us in that while we still were sinners Christ died for us" (Romans 5:8).

The gospel is good news because it reveals to me that I do not have to struggle desperately to save myself. On the one hand, I can't rescue myself from sin and death; I simply don't have the power to do it. On the other hand, there is no need for me even to try to earn salvation by my own merits; it has been given to me as a free gift. It's good news to be told that something has been given to us that we could not have obtained by our own efforts.

And yet the gospel does call for an effort from us—specifically, an effort to live our lives as followers of Christ. Paul refers to both the gift that has been given to us and the response that we should make to it: "As God's chosen ones, holy and beloved, clothe yourselves with compassion, kindness, humility, meekness, and patience" (Colossians 3:12). John likewise views our efforts to love as a response to the prior love of God for us: "We know love by this, that he laid down his life for us—and we ought to lay down our lives for one another" (1 John 3:16).

There *is* an element of "bad news" in the gospel. What Jesus has done for me is bad news for the sin within me, for my resistance to love. There is a part of me that must die on the cross with Jesus, in order that I may truly rise with him to eternal life. But just as the surgeon's knife in removing cancer brings life, so the love of Jesus would root out from within us all that causes death.

If we do not think of the gospel as good news, we are missing its most basic truths. If we do not think of ourselves as first of all sons and daughters of God, we are ignoring the heritage that has been given us. If we do not understand the primary message of Jesus as the assurance that God loves us, we have not heard him correctly, and we need to listen afresh to the good news the gospel has for us.

2. THE POWER OF GOD'S WORD

Paul, Silvanus, and Timothy, To the church of the Thessalonians in God the Father and the Lord Jesus Christ:
Grace to you and peace. . . .
We know, brothers and sisters beloved by God, that he has chosen you, because our message of the gospel came to you not in word only, but also in power and in the Holy Spirit and with full conviction.
—1 Thessalonians 1:1, 4-5

Paul's First Letter to the Thessalonians, sent in A.D. 50 or 51, was the first book of the New Testament to be written. Although the traditions underlying the gospels go back to the time of Jesus, they had yet to be written down in the form in which we read them in the gospels. So in one sense the opening words of Paul's first letter to the Thessalonians could be considered the opening words of the New Testament. It is striking that as opening words they tell us something important about the word of God.

After greeting the new converts in Thessalonica (converts made by Paul only a few months earlier) and commending them on their faith, hope, and charity (1 Thessalonians 1:2-3), Paul goes on to talk about what led to their conversion. The message that he had preached in their midst had not been merely a matter of words but a message with power, a message anointed by the Holy Spirit, a message producing conviction in those who heard it. Elsewhere Paul will speak about the signs and wonders and mighty works that accompanied and confirmed his preaching of the gospel (2 Corinthians 12:12), but here he speaks of a power intrinsic to the word of God, a power capable of calling forth faith. It was this power of the word that brought about the conversion of the Thessalonians.

Jesus also taught about the vitality and life-giving power of God's word. The parable of the sower and the seed was one illustration he used (Mark 4:3-8). Despite the adverse conditions that worked against producing a crop (rocky ground, thorns, birds, lack of rainfall), there was a bountiful harvest: thirty, sixty, a hundredfold. Luke's gospel makes clear the application of this parable: "The seed is the word of God" (Luke 8:11). Just as there is an inner life within a seed, waiting for the proper conditions so that it may burst forth, so there is a power and vitality in the word of God, waiting for someone to accept it so that it may develop and bear fruit. The farmer does not have to put life in the seed: it is already there. Neither do we have to strain to put power into the word of God. It is already there, waiting for us to tap it.

This power is found no less in the written word of God than in the oral message proclaimed by Paul. Through the inspiration of the Holy Spirit, the words of Scripture are God's words. They are addressed to us as much as to the early Christians. If we take God's word to heart, it can produce an abundant harvest within us. We should experience something of the inner quickening that the two disciples on the road to Emmaus experienced as they walked alongside Jesus and listened to his words (Luke 24:32).

How do we go about tapping the power of God's word? The first step is very simple: we need to read it. Simply acknowledging that the Bible is the word of God is not enough; we also have to make it a part of our lives. Unfortunately, many more people reverence the word of God from a distance than take it into their lives by their faithful reading.

The word of God is like seed sown in a field. The seed may have life within it, but it will only sprout and grow if the proper conditions are present. "But as for that in the good soil, these are the ones who, when they hear the word, hold it fast in an honest and good heart, and bear fruit with patient endurance" (Luke 8:15). We must welcome God's word with eagerness, taking it to heart; we must persevere in the word so that our lives will bear a rich harvest.

Our reading of Scripture must therefore be prayerful reading, reading as if we were in God's presence and he were speaking to us alone. We should submit ourselves to the word we read, accepting its truth and being willing to do what it requires of us. Not every page of the Bible will speak equally to us, but we should approach every page with reverence and an eagerness to hear what it will say to us.

Then we will experience what the Thessalonians experienced as Paul proclaimed the good news to them: the power of God operating through his word, the power of the Holy Spirit within us.

3. ACTING ON GOD'S WORD

As for you, mortal, your people who talk together about you by the walls, and at the doors of the houses, say to one another, each to a neighbor, "Come and hear what the word is that comes from the LORD." They come to you as people come, and they sit before you as my people, and they hear your words, but they will not obey them. For flattery is on their lips, but their heart is set on their gain. To them you are like a singer of love songs, one who has a beautiful voice and plays well on an instrument; they hear what you say, but they will not do it.

—Ezekiel 33:30-32

Prophets generally received a poor reception in ancient Israel. Amos, a southerner, was told in no uncertain terms that his prophetic ministry was unwelcome in the northern kingdom: "Go, flee away to the land of Judah, earn your bread there, and prophesy there" (Amos 7:12). Jeremiah's ministry was even less welcome; he was told, "You shall not prophesy in the name of the LORD, or you will die by our hand" (Jeremiah 11:21). When Jeremiah persisted in speaking God's word, he was beaten, put in stocks, and finally thrown into a well to die (20:2; 38:4-6).

In contrast to what happened to Amos and Jeremiah, Ezekiel had a rather easy time of it. He was not beaten or imprisoned; in fact, people came to hear what he had to say. But in the end, the word of God proclaimed through Ezekiel did not get much better reception than the word spoken through Amos and Jeremiah. For while the people said to each other, "Come and hear what the word is that comes from the LORD," they did nothing about it after they heard it. They listened to Ezekiel as they might listen to a popular singer—for entertainment. They may even have said afterward, "My, wasn't that a great performance Ezekiel put on tonight? I liked his lament over the fall of Tyre; it was very poetic."

The word of God spoken through Ezekiel found no home in them. By not responding to it, they rejected it as surely as others rejected the words of Amos and Jeremiah.

We are beset today by many of the same problems we read about in the Bible. We too hear God's word spoken to us in a variety of ways. Sometimes (but fortunately not very often) we simply reject it and refuse to listen to it. More often we acknowledge that it is God's word to us but do not respond to it as fully and completely as we should.

We go to Mass on Sunday and come away saying, "That was certainly a fine sermon Fr. Kelly gave today; you can tell he put a lot of work into it." Yet our lives go on afterward much the same as before. We acknowledge hearing a word from God but we do very little to act on it. As with those listening to Ezekiel, we show appreciation with our lips, but our hearts are set on our own way of life.

God doesn't send his word to us so that we might admire his performance in doing so. His word is meant to sink into us and change us in a radical and fundamental way. If we merely listen to what God says and thank him for speaking to us, but don't do anything about it, then we are rejecting his word as surely as it was rejected when proclaimed by Amos and Jeremiah.

James made the same point in his letter: "Be doers of the word, and not merely hearers who deceive themselves. For if any are hearers of the word and not doers, they are like those who look at themselves in a mirror; for they look at themselves and, on going away, immediately forget what they were like" (James 1:22-24). We must act on what we hear God saying to us if we are truly to receive God's word.

4. THE PARABLE OF THE SOWER

[Jesus said:] "A sower went out to sow. And as he sowed, some seeds fell on the path, and the birds came and ate them up. Other seeds fell on rocky ground, where they did not have much soil, and they sprang up quickly, since they had no depth of soil. But when the sun rose, they were scorched; and since they had no root, they withered away. Other seeds fell among thorns, and the thorns grew up and choked them. Other seeds fell on good soil and brought forth grain, some a hundredfold, some sixty, some thirty."

—Matthew 13:3-8

The parable of the sower conveys an important truth about the Christian life: Jesus does not merely invite us to find life in him but also to bear fruit.

There are some on whom the gospel message has little impact. Like seed dropped on a sidewalk and eaten by birds, the word of salvation never springs to life in them. And there are some who receive the gospel with eagerness and reorient their whole lives to following and serving Jesus. Their lives bear a rich harvest for the kingdom—thirty, sixty, a hundredfold.

Between these extremes are two other groups of people. Both eagerly receive the word at first, but bear no fruit. Both accept Jesus, but their lives do not produce the harvest that Jesus wants.

"As for what was sown on rocky ground, this is the one who hears the word and immediately receives it with joy; yet such a person has no root, but endures only for a while, and when trouble or persecution arises on account of the word, that person immediately falls away" (Matthew 13:20-21). Jesus does not say "*if* trouble arises" but "*when* trouble arises." Jesus teaches that the initial joy of becoming a Christian will not be enough to sustain a person through troubles, and there will be troubles. A deeper foundation is necessary, a foundation of commitment to God.

"As for what was sown among thorns, this is the one who hears the word, but the cares of the world and the lure of wealth choke the word, and it yields nothing" (Matthew

13:22). The word is initially taken to heart, but then the cares of the world sidetrack the person, and he or she ends up bearing no fruit.

What are the cares of the world? For some, it may be an overriding dedication to success that leaves no room in their lives for their family, for prayer, for Christian service. For others, it may be merely a preoccupation with trivia: spending excessive time on things that are not evil in themselves but that are a distraction to fruitfulness, whether they be sports or TV or hobbies. It is hard to have a life cluttered with distractions and still be a fruitful Christian.

The parable of the sower has particular application for our times. Many today are finding new life in the Spirit and receiving the word of God into their hearts with joy. But the test comes when their initial enthusiasm has subsided and they are confronted with trials and difficulties. A superficial joy at knowing Jesus will most often not be enough to sustain them through the hard times. Only a profound commitment of their lives to Jesus and his service will be enough. Joy is a fruit, not a foundation.

Many do make such a commitment to Jesus Christ and enter into his service with real dedication. But then difficult choices arise—decisions about priorities, about which activities must be dropped in order to have the time to serve Christ. With the pace of modern life and with the avalanche of distractions that our society provides (many of them perfectly harmless in themselves), we must choose where to devote our time, or our fruitfulness will be choked out by the cares and lures of the world. Fruitfulness requires that our activities be reexamined, our priorities reordered, our lives reshaped, so that we have the time and energy to serve God as he has called us to serve.

Jesus invites us to receive his word in our hearts, to commit ourselves to obeying it, to put our lives in order for his service, and to bear fruit—thirty, sixty, a hundredfold.

5. CASE STUDY: ADAM AND EVE

> Now the serpent was more crafty than any other wild animal that the LORD God had made. He said to the woman, "Did God say, 'You shall not eat from any tree in the garden'?" The woman said to the serpent, "We may eat of the fruit of the trees in the garden; but God said, 'You shall not eat of the fruit of the tree that is in the middle of the garden, nor shall you touch it, or you shall die.'" But the serpent said to the woman, "You will not die; for God knows that when you eat of it your eyes will be opened, and you will be like God, knowing good and evil." So when the woman saw that the tree was good for food, and that it was a delight to the eyes, and that the tree was to be desired to make one wise, she took of its fruit and ate; and she also gave some to her husband, who was with her, and he ate.
>
> —Genesis 3:1-6

The story of the first temptation and fall can teach us quite a bit about our own temptations and falls today. Through all the years the human race has been on the earth, human nature hasn't changed much, nor have the tactics of the tempter.

Adam and Eve knew quite clearly what God's law was for them—or at least they knew it when they weren't tempted to disobey it. God had clearly and unambiguously spoken his command to them, and Eve had no trouble remembering it when asked. But the serpent, the most crafty of animals, began its temptation in a most crafty way: "Did God say?" Did God *really* tell you not to eat the fruit of a certain tree? Is that what he *really* meant? Perhaps you misunderstood him. Or perhaps his command was for last week but not this week. Or again, he could have been suggesting an ideal to you, but not really imposing an absolute law that must be obeyed in every case. And then too, he is probably willing to make exceptions, because your case is really different, after all.

So temptation begins: Did God say? When we are not in a moment of temptation, God's laws are sufficiently clear to us. You shall not steal. You shall not commit adultery. But as we become tempted, their clarity erodes. Did God really say I shouldn't cheat on my income tax? It's not really stealing, is it? Did God forbid all sexual activity outside of marriage? Is he really concerned about this relationship I am entering into with another person?

In the moment of temptation we subtly convince ourselves that God's law isn't as we thought it was. In the moment of temptation, God's law becomes vague for us, full of obscurities and loopholes. In the moment of temptation, what was forbidden to us becomes very desirable—almost God's gift to us: "the woman saw that the tree was good . . . was a delight . . . was to be desired." As we succumb to temptation, we convince ourselves that we really aren't doing wrong, that we misunderstood God's law before, that God really doesn't mind what we are doing.

And so we fall into sin, just as the woman and the man in the garden fell the first time. The temptation presents itself to us, questions whether God really has forbidden it, and ends by assuring us that it must be permitted because we want to do it so badly.

These tactics of temptation are particularly effective today. Other people live by values and codes that tolerate conduct that God has forbidden. It is easier for us to ask, "Did God say?" when we can look around and find others indulging in the sins that tempt us.

What God's law says is usually not in doubt for us—unless we are tempted to disobey it. Then doubt comes to the fore: Did God say? The lesson of the man and the woman in the garden is sobering.

QUESTIONS FOR REFLECTION

1. Do you experience the gospel of Jesus Christ as good news for you? How would you summarize the basic message of the gospel? What verse in the four gospels is the most meaningful for you?

2. How often do you read the Bible? How much time do you usually spend reading it? Do you combine Scripture reading with prayer? What have you found to be the best way to reflect on God's words to you in Scripture?

3. What passage of Scripture has had the greatest impact on you, resulting in a change in your life? What is the greatest obstacle you face in bearing the fruit Jesus asks of you?

4. What lesson do you find in the fall of Eve and Adam? What are your most persistent temptations? What have you found to be the best way to resist them? How can God's word help you?

PART THREE

RESPONDING TO GOD'S CALL

I. JESUS, OUR LORD

[Jesus said:] "What do you think? A man had two sons; he went to the first and said, 'Son, go and work in the vineyard today.' He answered, 'I will not'; but later he changed his mind and went. The father went to the second and said the same; and he answered, 'I go, sir'; but he did not go. Which of the two did the will of his father?" They said, "The first."

—Matthew 21:28-31

Most of us have, at some point in our life, made a decision to serve the Lord. Depending on our background and the particular way God's call was addressed to us, we may think about our decision in different ways and express it in different terms. Some may think back to a time when they realized that God was real and that obeying him was eternally important. Some may have committed or dedicated themselves to God at a particular turning point in their lives. Others may remember a time of prayer in which they abandoned all they had, their future, and their very selves into the hands of God, for him to do with as he would. Still others can recall an occasion when they accepted Jesus into their lives as their Lord and Savior.

Such moments of decision and commitment made a marked difference in our lives. We felt somehow new; we became aware of a new power, a new freedom, a new joy. Problems that had been bothering us for years disappeared; we sensed the operation of grace in us. It seemed as if our previous life had been but a preparation for this moment, and that our subsequent life would be merely a living out of our new consciousness of ourselves as Christians.

We soon discovered that euphoria was not a fruit of the Spirit; that although some problems had disappeared, other problems remained, that it still took our own effort, as well as the winds of grace, to move us along the road of salvation. So we settled in for the long haul and set about living out our life as Christians. We realized that the moment of decision was only a moment, and that we could not dwell within it forever.

There is wisdom in this realization—but also danger. For with it comes a turning point in which we can continue to persevere as Christians or return to our former way of life. We can become like the second son who willingly said yes to his father but did not live out his yes. Chances are that this son was sincere when he told his father that he would work in the vineyard. He may well have meant to go but somehow got sidetracked. He may even have set out for the vineyard with fervor, but for one reason or another never arrived.

We too can set out to serve the Lord with fervor but slowly, step by step, change our direction. We can abandon everything into the hands of God, only to gradually and imperceptibly take it back into our own hands again. We can invite Jesus into our lives as our Lord and Savior, but over a period of time reassert ourselves as lord of our lives and come once again to rely on our own strength to save us.

Such a pattern is not inevitable, but there are precedents for it in Scripture. Did not the disciples leave all to follow Jesus, only to bicker about who was going to get the highest place (surely an exercise in self-assertion)? Did not one of the chosen twelve betray Jesus and another deny knowing him? Because of the danger of saying one thing and doing another, Jesus issued the warning, "Not everyone who says to me, 'Lord, Lord,' will enter the kingdom of heaven, but only the one who does the will of my Father in heaven" (Matthew 7:21).

It is not enough to have once cried out to Jesus, "You are my Lord": we must make this our decision and prayer every day. It is not enough to have once placed everything in the hands of God; we must place there again anything that we find ourselves taking back.

Our previous commitments of ourselves to God have made a difference in who we are. These commitments have been the occasion for the grace of God to be given to us, and indeed they were a response to his grace. But grace demands our continued cooperation. Every day we must reissue the invitation to Jesus to be our Lord, and then behave accordingly.

2. THE CALL TO REPENTANCE

From that time Jesus began to proclaim, "Repent, for the kingdom of heaven has come near."

—Matthew 4:17

When we think of repentance, we usually think of forsaking sin. If there is serious sin in our life, we hear the call to repent as a call to commit that sin no longer. While repentance certainly involves a change of behavior, it involves something much more fundamental, as well.

Repentance is a translation of a Greek word used in Scripture, *metanoia*. Metanoia means a change of mind, a change of heart. It thus means something deeper than a change in our external actions: it means a change within ourselves, a change in the underlying source of our behavior. It means a change of our orientation, our way of thinking, our values and priorities. It means adopting a new goal for our lives—a goal that determines how we act.

The radical nature of the call to repentance is made clear by Jesus: "He called the crowd with his disciples, and said to them, 'If any want to become my followers, let them deny themselves and take up their cross and follow me. For those who want to save their life will lose it, and those who lose their life for my sake, and for the sake of the gospel, will save it. For what will it profit them to gain the whole world and forfeit their life?'" (Mark 8:34-36).

Jesus demands a reversal of our normal way of thinking and our instinctive values. We are inclined to want the best for ourselves, to place our good before that of others, to weigh every decision in terms of the benefits for us. Even if our lives are not completely dominated by the urge to acquire money and possessions, we can still succumb to the childish temptation to want the biggest cookie on the plate of life. Even if we are not ruthless in our pursuit of getting ahead, we still have a hard time putting the success of others ahead of our own.

The repentance Jesus calls for is a reorientation of this instinctive urge to put ourselves first. Jesus calls for a conversion from relying on our own talents and resources to relying on his care for us. Repentance means making *him* the Lord of our lives instead of ourselves.

If we understand Jesus' call to repentance in this way, some of his other teachings take on added significance. The drive to accumulate wealth can be seen as an expression of self-sufficiency, a desire to make one's future secure against all dangers. But this is as much folly as trying to march a camel through the eye of a needle. Recall the parable of the rich fool, who decided to build larger barns to store his goods for his own future security, only to have his life taken from him that very night (Luke 12:16-21). True security lies not in what we possess but in what we give up; true security lies not in reliance on our own resources but in reliance on Jesus Christ.

Repentance is a reorientation of our lives. Repentance is grasping hold of the paradoxical truth that the one who would save her or his life must embrace the loss of it. Repentance is reversing our instinctive set of priorities and living according to the values that Jesus taught.

The call to repentance therefore goes much deeper than turning aside from obvious sins. The need for repentance is a lifelong need, because it is the process of continually placing our lives in the hands of God. It is the ongoing process of putting Jesus and his kingdom first in our daily decisions and in the long-range direction of our lives, in our thoughts and in our desires. Repentance is the daily taking up of the cross of Jesus so that we may follow in his footsteps.

3. DOING THE IMPOSSIBLE

> The angel said to her, "Do not be afraid, Mary, for you have found favor with God. And now, you will conceive in your womb and bear a son, and you will name him Jesus." . . . Mary said to the angel, "How can this be, since I am a virgin?" The angel said to her, "The Holy Spirit will come upon you, and the power of the Most High will overshadow you; therefore the child to be born will be holy; he will be called Son of God. And now, your relative Elizabeth in her old age has also conceived a son; and this is the sixth month for her who was said to be barren. For nothing will be impossible with God."
> —Luke 1:30-31, 34-37

Neither Elizabeth nor Mary was a likely candidate for motherhood. Elizabeth was long past her childbearing years. It would seem impossible for her to conceive a child in her old age, when she had been unable to do so in her youth. Mary was betrothed but not married. She didn't dismiss the angel's promise that she would bear a son, but neither did she see how it was possible. The angel assured her, however, that nothing was impossible for God—neither her conceiving a child in her virginity nor Elizabeth's bearing a son in her old age.

The mission of Jesus was rooted in the impossible from the moment of his conception in Mary's womb. He was fully human but not merely fully human. He was the eternal Word of God become flesh in our midst. He knew hunger, thirst, and fatigue, but he restored sight to the blind and hearing to the deaf and raised the dead to life. He did what was humanly impossible because as the Son of God he shared in God's power.

Jesus not only did the impossible but asked the impossible as well. He healed the sick and told his followers to do likewise. He walked on water and invited Peter to join him. He wasn't teaching Peter a better way to cross the lake, but rather challenging his faith—his willingness to follow Jesus wherever he might beckon, however impossible that might seem.

The disciples didn't find Jesus' requirements easy. They must have silently winced as he proclaimed a new standard, one that was even more stringent than the law of Moses. They didn't find the old law easy to keep; so how did Jesus expect them to live up to the greater demands of the new law? If the requirements of the kingdom are as Jesus proclaims, then who can ever meet them? "Who can be saved?" they exclaimed. Jesus replied, "What is impossible for mortals is possible for God" (Luke 18:26-27). His words are an echo of the angel's words to Mary.

Jesus asks that we imitate him. But how can we love with his totally self-sacrificing love, if we do not in some sense become him? Paul could boldly state, "It is no longer I who live, but it is Christ who lives in me" (Galatians 2:20). Yet such a transformation seems to be beyond us. It seems no more possible for Jesus to be born in us than it seemed possible to Mary for him to be conceived in her. Even if we are willing to let Christ live in us, we know how stubbornly our self-will clings to life and how desperately it resists relinquishing itself for another. We know what Jesus is asking us to do, but we nevertheless ask, "How can this be?" The answer we receive is the same: "What is impossible for you is possible for God."

God makes it possible for us to live in Jesus, but our own faith and effort must also play a role. When Peter began to doubt that he could safely walk on water and began to sink, Jesus rebuked him for his lack of faith. When a man full of both hope and doubt brought his afflicted son to Jesus to be cured, Jesus demanded faith of him, telling him, "All things can be done for the one who believes." The man replied with a cry that many of us have prayed ourselves: "I believe; help my unbelief!" (Mark 9:23-24). And when the disciples asked why they weren't able to cast out a demon, Jesus answered that it was because they had so little faith: "Truly I tell you, if you have faith the size of a mustard seed, you will say to this mountain, 'Move from here to there,' and it will move; and nothing will be impossible for you" (Matthew 17:20). If nothing is impossible for God, neither is anything impossible for faith.

We may think that the faith to move mountains is an impossible faith, a level of faith far beyond us. And we are right. Our faith, our cooperation with God's power, is itself a gift from him. But God wants to give the gift of faith to us so that the impossible might be done in our lives. He wants Christ's life to become our life—a miracle far greater than moving a mountain. He wants to overshadow us with his Holy Spirit so that Christ will live in us.

4. GOD WANTS US ANYWAY

> Now the disciples had forgotten to bring any bread; and they had only one loaf with them in the boat. And he cautioned them, saying, "Watch out—beware of the yeast of the Pharisees and the yeast of Herod." They said to one another, "It is because we have no bread." And becoming aware of it, Jesus said to them, "Why are you talking about having no bread? Do you still not perceive or understand? Are your hearts hardened? . . . When I broke the five loaves for the five thousand, how many baskets full of broken pieces did you collect?" They said to him, "Twelve." . . . Then he said to them, "Do you not yet understand?"
>
> —Mark 8:14-17, 19, 21

The gospel portrait of the first followers of Jesus is, on the whole, an unflattering picture. The gospels do record professions of faith in Christ: Peter's, "You are the Messiah, the Son of the living God" (Matthew 16:16), and Martha's, "I believe that you are the Messiah, the Son of God, the one coming into the world" (John 11:27). But there are also many instances where the faith of Jesus' followers was weak, where they were slow to understand his message, where they were ruled by fear.

Sometimes the disciples failed to understand the teachings of Jesus. They had to approach him privately to have him explain the meaning of parables (Matthew 13:36). They were sometimes shocked by his message: "When the disciples heard this, they were greatly astounded and said, 'Then who can be saved?'" (19:25). And they were very slow to understand his coming death and resurrection. Luke recounts three different times that Jesus foretold his coming passion (Luke 9:22, 44; 18:31-33). Yet even after the third explanation, the disciples "understood nothing about all these things; in fact, what he said was hidden from them, and they did not grasp what was said" (18:34).

The dullness of the disciples continued to the end. Luke recounts that at the Last Supper, even after Jesus had shared his body and blood with them, they fell into a dispute over which of them was the most important (Luke 22:24). Jesus tried to warn Peter that he would be severely tested, but Peter brushed his words aside with bluster and bravado (22:31-33). Jesus told the disciples to be ready for a time of crisis, and they reassured him that they were indeed prepared for it because they had two swords—misunderstanding the nature of the coming trial (22:36-38).

It is as if Jesus had not picked the most qualified and promising people to be his disciples, but had instead simply asked people at random to follow him. Normally the leader of a new cause will want to assemble the best talent; Jesus, on the other hand, seemed to select a group of people who were at best unremarkable. The Pharisees dismissed the friends of Jesus as a scruffy lot, "tax collectors and sinners" (Luke 7:34); their judgment was not off the mark.

And that is good news for us. No matter how slow we seem to be in growing to maturity in our faith, no matter how frail we seem to ourselves, no matter how discouraged we become, we are in good company. The first followers that Jesus chose were no more adept at following him than we are. They found eternal life, not because they earned it, but because Jesus freely gave it to them.

Jesus has also chosen us and offers us eternal life. No doubt he could have chosen more competent people. But, despite our weaknesses and failings, he chose us.

5. SELF-SACRIFICING LOVE

> Slaves, accept the authority of your masters with all deference, not only those who are kind and gentle but also those who are harsh. For it is a credit to you if, being aware of God, you endure pain while suffering unjustly. If you endure when you are beaten for doing wrong, what credit is that? But if you endure when you do right and suffer for it, you have God's approval. For to this you have been called, because Christ also suffered for you, leaving you an example, so that you should follow in his steps.
>
> —1 Peter 2:18-21

The New Testament's teaching regarding slaves is not very palatable to us today. Slaves are to "be submissive to their masters and to give satisfaction in every respect; they are not to talk back" (Titus 2:9). They are to "regard their masters as worthy of all honor" (1 Timothy 6:1). Slaves are to work hard to please their masters and not slack off when no one is watching (Ephesians 6:5-7; Colossians 3:22-23). They are even to put up with undeserved punishment, according to the First Letter of Peter.

Although there may be no distinction between slave and free in Christ (Galatians 3:28), the New Testament does not directly advocate the abolition of slavery. Quite the contrary: it urges slaves to accept their condition, even under harsh masters. Not even Paul's letter to Philemon, a slave owner, challenges the basic institution of slavery.

This view is shocking to us today. We expect the church to be a champion of human and civil rights. We expect Christians to be involved in the political and social institutions of the world, working to improve them according to Christian values. We take it for granted that slavery is evil and abhorrent; we would be shocked to read a church document that tolerated slavery today.

Yet the New Testament doesn't condemn slavery as immoral, and it repeatedly urges slaves to be obedient to their masters. What are we to make of this?

One response is to take what the Bible says as culturally conditioned: the writers of the Old and New Testaments reflect the values and customs of their times, and allowance has to be made for that. Paul was uncritically accepting the common practice of slavery in the culture in which he wrote. Today we live in a different culture and are better able to understand the application of certain Christian principles.

This type of response has a danger, however. While understanding the cultural settings in which Scripture was written can help us understand its meaning, care must be taken lest the teachings of Scripture be cavalierly dismissed as culturally conditioned when they challenge our own way of life. Almost any commandment or difficult teaching could be written off on the grounds that it goes against the grain today.

Nor does an appeal to cultural conditioning fully explain the teaching of the New Testament regarding slaves. No culture holds up innocent suffering as something to be accepted. It was not the common practice when the First Letter of Peter was written for slaves to willingly and patiently accept undeserved punishment. But this was what slaves were asked to do in imitation of Christ. The cross of Christ—rather than the prevailing culture—is the key to understanding Peter's teaching about slaves.

The message of the gospel transcends and challenges every culture. Paul preached Christ crucified: a scandal to Jews, madness to pagans, and an absurdity by the values of modern society. The cross occupies an inescapably central place in Christian belief, making imitation of Christ the ultimate challenge for everyone—Jew or Greek, slave or free, male or female.

Slavery is indeed evil and abhorrent, but there was little that early Christians could have done to challenge such a widely accepted and deeply entrenched institution. However, the message of Christianity is so radical in its call for death to self that even slavery and unwarranted suffering are of secondary importance. It is not only slaves who are to lay down their lives in profound imitation of Christ: we all must. We can apply Peter's words to ourselves in whatever situation we find ourselves and read them as an exhortation to self-sacrificing love: "For to this you have been called, because Christ also suffered for you, leaving you an example, so that you should follow in his steps" (1 Peter 2:21).

6. SIMPLE THINGS

> Elisha sent a messenger to him, saying, "Go, wash in the Jordan seven times, and your flesh shall be restored and you shall be clean." But Naaman became angry and went away. . . . But his servants approached and said to him, "Father, if the prophet had commanded you to do something difficult, would you not have done it? How much more, when all he said to you was, 'Wash, and be clean'?" So he went down and immersed himself seven times in the Jordan, according to the word of the man of God; his flesh was restored like the flesh of a young boy.
>
> —2 Kings 5:10-11, 13-14

Naaman was a Syrian army commander afflicted with leprosy. He went to the prophet Elisha in Israel to seek healing. But Elisha didn't heal him or prescribe a difficult cure for him; Elisha simply sent word to him to bathe seven times in the Jordan River. Naaman was offended; were not the rivers of Syria better than the rivers of Israel? (2 Kings 5:12). Naaman had expected something better from the prophet than to be told to bathe in the Jordan—a rather small and sometimes muddy river.

Naaman's servants persuaded him to obey Elisha anyway. If Naaman would have been willing to do something far more difficult than what Elisha asked, he could at least perform this simple task. And when Naaman obeyed the prophet's simple command, he was healed of his leprosy.

Most of the things that Christ asks us to do are rather simple; some of them are even boring. But our obedience to the simple commands of Christ will make as much difference in our lives as Naaman's obedience made in his.

Jesus instructed his followers to forgive each other without limit. It is usually not complicated to forgive someone who has wronged us, but it is a simple thing that we can find very difficult to do.

"Peace be with you" was the risen Jesus' greeting to his followers (John 20:19). They were to be peaceful because they were sons and daughters of his Father in heaven and therefore didn't need to be worried or anxious about their lives (Matthew 6:25-34). But we have trouble maintaining this simple perspective and so fall into worry and anxiety and depression.

It is a simple thing to get up half an hour earlier in the morning and devote ourselves to Scripture reading and prayer or to set aside regular time each day for communion with God. Yet the impact of this simple commitment is profound. Our daily faithfulness bears fruit out of all proportion to the effort we put into it.

We may daydream about doing heroic things for God, and yet be reluctant to do the simple, if mundane, things he asks of us. Few of us are called to move halfway around the world to serve God; all of us are called to love and serve people right where we are. We may not be called to sacrifice our lives for our faith, yet all of us are called to sacrifice a portion of our time in service of our fellow human beings.

Faithfulness to the simple commands and invitations of Jesus is as important as faithfulness in great things. Faithfulness in the simple things of each day bears dramatic fruit in a transformed life, as miraculous as Naaman's rising clean from a simple dunking in the waters of the Jordan.

7. TALENTS

[Jesus said:] "For it is as if a man, going on a journey, summoned his slaves and entrusted his property to them; to one he gave five talents, to another two, to another one, to each according to his ability. Then he went away. The one who had received the five talents went off at once and traded with them, and made five more talents. In the same way, the one who had the two talents made two more talents. But the one who had received the one talent went off and dug a hole in the ground and hid his master's money."

—Matthew 25:14-18

We are familiar with how this parable turns out. The slaves who made use of their master's talents were praised and rewarded. The slave who buried his talent was condemned, for he could at least have put the money in the bank and earned interest. And we know in a general way how this parable applies to us: we are to make use of the "talents" that God has given us for the sake of his kingdom.

There seems to be another side to the story, however. The slave who received only one talent was not a man of great abilities; that is why his master entrusted the smallest sum to him. We might imagine this slave deliberating about what to do with his talent: "I could try trading with it in the hope of making a profit. But then again, I might lose it if things don't turn out right. My master would be furious with me. I could put it in the bank. But what would happen if it were embezzled or the bank failed? There is so much about business and economics that I don't understand! No, I had better play it safe and bury it. I won't gain anything that way, but I can be sure that I won't lose anything, either."

The master condemned this slave as "wicked and lazy" and dismissed him from his service (Matthew 25:26, 30). We may find the master's action harsh. After all, the slave didn't steal the money; he was simply afraid to do anything with it. He knew that he was a man of limited abilities and played it safe.

Jesus, however, approves of the master's action. After all, if the master had wanted his money buried, he could have done it himself and not bothered entrusting it to his slaves. The very fact that he put his money in the care of his slaves meant that he was willing to let them take risks with it. The master knew that one of his slaves was a man of limited abilities, but wanted him to make the best use of those abilities that he could. The master probably would have forgiven the slave for entering into a business deal that went sour, but he had little patience with his being so fearful that he refused to take even the risk involved in putting the money in the bank.

It is also noteworthy that the master didn't give his slaves explicit instructions about what to do with the talents he gave them. He did not say to one, "Go into the shipping business," and to another, "Open up a clothing store." He left it up to them how they would invest their talents but expected them to make the best use of them that they could.

God treats us much the same. He equips us for service to his kingdom but usually doesn't dictate to us precisely how we should serve. Unless God gives us some special guidance, he expects us to choose the way that seems best to us and then to work as hard as we can as his servants.

God also expects us to take risks. There is no absolutely safe way to make it through life. Deciding where to go to school, choosing an occupation, making a commitment to another person—all involve risk. Whenever we give ourselves fully, we risk disappointment, or failure, or rejection. Yet without risk, there is also no possibility of reward. We can respond to these risks fearfully by avoiding any commitment or giving of ourselves. Or we can respond in faith, trusting that the Lord will oversee our service to him, and opening ourselves to the enormous possibilities of what we can accomplish if only we try.

God may not dictate the precise way to use our talents, but he does expect us to use them on his behalf. He will forgive our mistakes if we do our best, but he will be less patient with us if we are so fearful and untrusting that we hold back from his service. The parable of the talents teaches us about faith in action.

8. CUNNING AS SERPENTS

When Paul noticed that some were Sadducees and others were Pharisees, he called out in the council, "Brothers, I am a Pharisee, a son of Pharisees. I am on trial concerning the hope of the resurrection of the dead." When he said this, a dissension began between the Pharisees and the Sadducees, and the assembly was divided. (The Sadducees say that there is no resurrection, or angel, or spirit; but the Pharisees acknowledge all three.) Then a great clamor arose, and certain scribes of the Pharisees' group stood up and contended, "We find nothing wrong with this man. What if a spirit or an angel has spoken to him?" When the dissension became violent, the tribune, fearing that they would tear Paul to pieces, ordered the soldier to go down, take him by force, and bring him into the barracks.

—Acts 23:6-10

This remarkable scene takes place at the end of Paul's missionary travels, after his arrival in Jerusalem and arrest. He will remain under arrest for the next two years and then be taken to Rome to have his case heard by the Roman emperor. But at the moment, he is appearing before the Jewish council, the Sanhedrin, in Jerusalem.

The Sanhedrin included members from two different Jewish groups. One group was the Sadducees, a conservative aristocratic elite who placed great weight on the five books of Moses, Genesis through Deuteronomy. The other group was the Pharisees, who accepted religious beliefs that developed after the books of Moses were written. Sadducees and Pharisees disagreed about many matters, with the Pharisees believing in a resurrection from the dead and in recent speculations about angels and spirits, while the Sadducees denied the resurrection and did not accept speculations about angels and spirits. Paul was raised and trained as a Pharisee.

Paul had been arrested for proclaiming the gospel of Jesus Christ and now stood before the Sanhedrin for his Christian beliefs. But Paul's defense of himself is surprising and shrewd. He says nothing about Jesus Christ, but instead claims that he is on trial for his beliefs as a Pharisee! Now, it was true that both Pharisees and followers of Christ looked forward to a resurrection, but for Paul to claim that he was being tried for his belief in the resurrection as a Pharisee was certainly far from the whole truth.

Paul's claim had its desired effect. Instead of being united against him, the Sadducees and the Pharisees started arguing with each other, and some Pharisees even began to assert

Paul's innocence! The scene has its comic elements. Finally Paul is rescued by Roman authorities, in whose hands he evidently felt safer.

What are we to make of this scene? Did Paul back down from the gospel to save his own hide? Or was this a case of a Christian not being required to bear suffering that could be avoided without compromising any fundamental beliefs?

Two gospel passages may give us insights. First, Jesus promised that the Holy Spirit would give words to his followers when they were hauled before councils, so they were not to worry about what they would say (Matthew 10:17-20). If his promise was not fulfilled in such a great apostle as Paul, it is hard to see who could qualify for it. And if it was fulfilled in him, then Paul's defense must have been inspired!

Second, in Matthew's gospel, immediately preceding the promise of the Spirit's inspiration of disciples in courtrooms, is the verse: "I am sending you out like sheep into the midst of wolves; so be wise [*cunning* in some translations] as serpents and innocent as doves" (Matthew 10:16). Paul's defense of himself before the Sanhedrin was certainly cunning. In fact we would be hard-pressed to find an example of greater Christian cunning in the Book of Acts.

When we are in situations in which others are hostile to us because of our beliefs, we can rely on Jesus' promise that we will receive help from the Holy Spirit. Yet we can also keep the example of Paul in mind. In this particular instance he did not feel obliged to bring persecution down on himself. And in fact he went on to accomplish a great deal as a witness for Christ because his "hide" was still intact. There are times to bear fearless witness and there are times when that is not demanded of us—perhaps because of the good we will accomplish in other ways. We can pray for the guidance of the Holy Spirit to help us discern which times are which.

9. CASE STUDY: MOSES THE RELUCTANT

[God said:] "So come, I will send you to Pharaoh to bring my people, the Israelites, out of Egypt." But Moses said to God, "Who am I that I should go to Pharaoh and bring the Israelites out of Egypt?" . . .

But Moses said to God, "What shall I say to them?" . . .

Then Moses answered, "But suppose they do not believe me?" . . .

But Moses said to the LORD, "O my Lord, I have never been eloquent . . . but I am slow of speech and slow of tongue." . . .

But he said, "O my Lord, please send someone else." . . .

But Moses spoke to the LORD, "The Israelites have not listened to me; how then shall Pharaoh listen to me, poor speaker that I am?"

—Exodus 3:10-11, 13; 4:1, 10, 13; 6:12

One of the most discouraging aspects of our Christian lives can be our awareness that we are not responding to God's call to us as we should. It can be sobering to look back over our lives and realize that our progress has been uneven and slow. We may remember specific instances in which we didn't respond to an invitation from God and wonder how our lives would be different now if we had.

We can also be pained by our awareness that we are not responding to God right now as we should. Perhaps we hear the word of the Lord addressed to us through Scripture or through a homily but don't experience the word sinking into us and having an impact. Sometimes we can't even remember afterward what Scripture passage was read or what the homilist said. At other times we may experience a resistance in ourselves to what we hear—a hardness of heart that turns away God's word.

Such an awareness can give rise to discouragement: "I have always been this way—halfhearted, uncertain, lukewarm—and I'm afraid I always will be." We see others around us eagerly responding to God's call; we wish we were as quick and wholehearted in our response.

Scripture was written for our encouragement as well as our instruction. This encouragement is often conveyed through the lives of those whom God has called in the past.

Moses was the greatest leader of the Old Testament. His work, more than that of any other, was responsible for transforming the descendents of Abraham into the people of God. Yet Moses' response to God's call was not always eager and wholehearted. In the Old Testament account Moses repeatedly argued with God, trying to get out of doing the service God asked of him. Moses objected that he didn't have the gifts to do what God wanted, and he pleaded with God to "please send someone else." We may have had similar conversations in prayer when we felt that we weren't quite up to the challenge of what God seemed to be asking of us.

If God could carry out his greatest work before the coming of Christ through such a reluctant servant as Moses, he can carry out his will through us despite our uneven response. That's not to say that our response isn't important, but rather that God doesn't depend on our perfection. God asks us to make whatever response we are able to, while giving us the capability to grow in our response through his love.

God's invitation is not an impossible standard that we could never meet; God does not want his message to discourage us. God is saying to us, "Take heart! I did great things with Moses, and I can do great things even with you. Don't center your attention on your own shortcomings. Focus on my love, and move on with me."

QUESTIONS FOR REFLECTION

1. Have you ever experienced a turning point in your relationship with God? What immediate impact did it have on you? What is its impact today?

2. Do you ever marvel that God chose *you*? That God loves *you*? That God invites *you* to everlasting life? If you sometimes find these truths difficult to believe, what could help you better internalize them?

3. What are the simple things Jesus asks of you? What is the most difficult thing he has asked you to do? What might he be asking of you now, so that you may follow more closely in his footsteps?

4. What are the particular gifts and talents that God has given you? What are you doing to use them in his service? What is the greatest risk you have taken through faith?

5. Have you ever pleaded with God to get out of what he was asking of you? What was the outcome? What encouragement do you find in the story of Moses?

PART FOUR

THE FAMILY OF GOD

I. LIKE LITTLE CHILDREN

> People were bringing little children to him in order that he might touch them; and the disciples spoke sternly to them. But when Jesus saw this, he was indignant and said to them, "Let the little children come to me; do not stop them; for it is to such as these that the kingdom of God belongs. Truly I tell you, whoever does not receive the kingdom of God as a little child will never enter it."
>
> —Mark 10:13-15

Jesus' words must have startled the disciples: not only were little children to be welcomed into his presence, but they were to enjoy a privileged place in the kingdom of God. In fact, Jesus bluntly warned his followers, "Truly I tell you, unless you change and become like children, you will never enter the kingdom of heaven" (Matthew 18:3).

Since Jesus' words indicate a basic requirement for salvation, it is well worth pondering their meaning. Often we focus on the qualities that we presume characterize children and try to imitate them in our lives. Children are thought to be innocent, without guile, direct in their affections, loving, trusting, spontaneous in their emotions, joyful, and carefree. We in turn try to make these characteristics a part of our lives, usually without complete success.

Parents know that these traits do characterize children. But as any parent knows, there is another side to the story. Children can also be self-centered, inconsiderate, prey to petty jealousies, indiscriminate in their affections, and inconsistent in their behavior. So how could Jesus have made childlike behavior a requirement for entering the kingdom of God?

If we situate these words of Jesus in the context of his other teachings, however, its meaning becomes clearer. The essential characteristic of children that Jesus would have us focus on is their status as sons and daughters. A child is a child of parents. Whatever the character traits of children might be, whatever stage of moral development they might have attained, the life of small children is essentially defined in terms of their relationship with their parents. Nothing can change that basic relationship.

The relationship of parent and child underlies the parable of the prodigal son (Luke 15:11-32). The prodigal did not act as a good son should have; even after he repented, he thought that the most he could possibly ask of his father was to return to his house as a servant. But the father nevertheless insisted that he was indeed his son and gave him a full welcome home. How the prodigal behaved did not change the basic reality that he was his father's son, nor did his behavior change his father's love for him.

Jesus taught us to pray to God as "our Father"; through the Holy Spirit we are adopted children of God. "God has sent the Spirit of his Son into our hearts, crying, 'Abba! Father!'" (Galatians 4:6).

Fundamental to being a Christian is the relationship that Jesus has established between us and his Father: we are daughters and sons of God. Our first response must be to acknowledge that relationship and enter more fully into it.

Interpreted in this light, Jesus is not urging us to adopt childlike character traits in our life, much less to act childishly. He is urging us to accept the sonship and daughtership his Father is giving us. He is saying most solemnly that unless we enter into our sonship or daughtership, we will not be part of the kingdom of God. The kingdom of God is the family of the Father, made up of those who have received adoption through the Spirit of Christ.

2. GOD'S ADOPTED CHILDREN

[God] chose us in Christ before the foundation of the world to be holy and blameless before him in love. He destined us for adoption as his children through Jesus Christ, according to the good pleasure of his will, to the praise of his glorious grace that he freely bestowed on us in the Beloved.

—Ephesians 1:4-6

Jesus taught about his Father's love for us by comparing it to human love. To show us that our heavenly Father desires to hear our prayers, he used the example of a parent and a child: "Is there anyone among you who, if your child asks for bread, will give a stone? Or if the child asks for a fish, will give a snake? If you then, who are evil, know how to give good gifts to your children, how much more will your Father in heaven give good things to those who ask him!" (Matthew 7:9-11).

Jesus told the parable of the prodigal son to teach about his Father's willingness to welcome us back when we are repentant, no matter how seriously we have sinned against him. Jesus said in effect, "Consider how much you love your children, and believe that God your Father loves you even more."

We are not simply God's children, however; we are his adopted children. Jesus is the firstborn Son of the Father; we are his brothers and sisters through adoption. Can we learn anything about our relationship with God by reflecting on the relationship between adoptive parents and adopted children?

The first thing that we might note about adoption is that the initiative lies with the parents, not with the children. Children are adopted because parents decide to adopt them, sometimes deciding before an infant is born that they want to adopt a child, and then waiting for a child to be born who needs an adoptive home.

This fact about human adoption is reflected in the divine order also. The fundamental fact about our relationship with God is that he acted first. "You did not choose me but I chose you," Jesus told his disciples at the Last Supper (John 15:16). Similarly the Letter to the Ephesians proclaims that "God chose us in Christ before the foundation of the world" and "destined us for adoption as his children" (Ephesians 1:4-5) God's choice of us was made long before we were born—even before the world was made.

Although adopted children are chosen by their parents, this does not mean that there is no decision for them to make. As adopted children become older, they must decide to truly accept their adoptive parents as their parents. This is a decision an adoptive parent cannot make for them. A parent can decide to adopt, but the child must ratify that adoption, so to speak, if the relationship between them is to endure into adulthood. So too in our relationship with God. He may have chosen us from all eternity, but we must accept that choice if we are to truly enter into a relationship with him.

Adopted children are sometimes insecure and wonder whether they are really loved. They are tempted to believe that it is through some fault of their own that they are not being raised by their biological parents. They are more susceptible to feeling rejected, more prone to fears of not belonging. Parents who adopt know that such temptations are inevitable, and they therefore make extra efforts to demonstrate their love for their adopted child. They will go out of their way to reassure adopted children that they are wanted and do truly belong.

Many of us are tempted to believe that we are not really loved by God, and for good reason; because of our sins, we fear that we are not very lovable. We are tempted to believe that God's adoption of us was conditional: if we lead faultless lives, God will keep us, but otherwise he will banish us into the outer darkness. Sometimes we do not feel very secure in God's love. Yet God loves us even if we are not completely lovable. "God proves his love for us in that while we still were sinners Christ died for us" (Romans 5:8).

God's love for us is a gift; we are his children because he chose us. His love is more complete and unconditional than even the human love of a parent for a child. As his adopted children we can be secure in his love and know that he is truly our Father.

3. GOD'S INSTRUMENTS ON EARTH

Oh, that you would tear open the heavens
        and come down,
    so that the mountains would quake at
        your presence—
as when fire kindles brushwood
    and the fire causes water to boil—
to make your name known to your adversaries,
    so that the nations might tremble at your presence!
                                            —Isaiah 64:1-2

Chapters 63 and 64 of the Book of Isaiah contain a psalm-like lament apparently written sometime after the destruction of Jerusalem and its temple in 586 B.C. and the exile of its inhabitants to Babylon. The psalm laments the condition of the chosen people, asking why the tragedy of the exile happened. Why had God allowed his people to stray from him? Why had God allowed the destruction of his temple? "Your holy cities have become a wilderness. . . . Our holy and beautiful house [i.e., the temple], where our ancestors praised you, has been burned. . . . After all this, will you restrain yourself, O LORD? Will you keep silent, and punish us so severely?" (Isaiah 64:10-12).

The psalm begs God to be present in power, to clearly demonstrate his dominion by signs and wonders, to "tear open the heavens and come down," tossing aside mountains, making the world tremble at God's awesome manifestation of himself. The lament asks God to work unheard-of miracles, removing all doubt of his lordship over the earth.

It is easy to long for the same kind of demonstration of the power of God today. Many today do not acknowledge the existence of God or the lordship of Jesus. And some followers of Jesus seem disheartened and lukewarm. If God is the Creator of the universe, couldn't he level a few mountain ranges as a demonstration of his power? Couldn't he work some cosmic sign to prove his existence to the skeptical and indifferent? Couldn't he loose a few thunderbolts to bolster the faith of his followers?

God did end the exile of his chosen people and bring them back to Jerusalem, but he accomplished this through human instruments. He did not move mountains to demonstrate his power; he did not destroy the walls of Babylon with a thunderbolt to free his people. Instead he made use of a Persian king, Cyrus, who captured Babylon and allowed the exiles to return home. God made use of men like Nehemiah to restore the walls of Jerusalem.

And although Jesus worked miracles during his public ministry, his emphasis was on forming disciples rather than on demonstrating to the masses that he was indeed the Son of God. If his followers could have prayed with faith to cast a mountain into the sea (Mark 11:23), surely Jesus could have used signs and wonders, if he wanted, to silence his opponents or win over the indifferent. But Jesus chose to carry out his mission by forming a people. He chose to have his Spirit remain present in the world in the lives of men and women.

God chooses to work through human instruments to demonstrate his power. The sign of God's presence is the love that exists among his followers. In God's plan, we are to be his miracles in the world today.

4. WITNESSES TO THE TRUTH

[Peter said:] "We are witnesses to all that he did both in Judea and in Jerusalem. They put him to death by hanging him on a tree; but God raised him on the third day and allowed him to appear, not to all the people but to us who were chosen by God as witnesses, and who ate and drank with him after he rose from the dead."

—Acts 10:39-41

Jesus' plan was to have the good news about himself spread by witnesses. For this purpose he invited certain men and women to be his followers—to literally follow after him as he traveled about Galilee and Judea. He spent time instructing them, but mostly he just spent time with them. Their education was less a matter of formal lectures than of simply being with Jesus and getting to know him. This was the group that Jesus began to gather around himself at the beginning of his public ministry, and it was chiefly to this group that he appeared after his resurrection from the dead.

The task of this group of followers was to bear witness to what they had observed while Jesus was with them. They were to report on their firsthand knowledge, on "what we have heard, what we have seen with our eyes, what we have looked at and touched with our hands. . . . We declare to you what we have seen and heard" (1 John 1:1, 3).

Thus, when it came time to replace Judas among the twelve, his successor had to be among those who had "accompanied us during all the time that the Lord Jesus went in and out among us, beginning from the baptism of John until the day when he was taken up from us—one of these must become a witness with us to his resurrection" (Acts 1:21-22).

Why did Jesus choose to have the good news of his resurrection spread by a small band of witnesses? Why didn't Jesus appear to the crowds after his resurrection and instruct thousands, as he did before his death? Surely his coming back from the dead would have been a sensation, and it would have been easy for him to attract huge crowds. Would not the church have gotten off to a faster start this way? Why did Jesus choose the slower and more indirect method of appearing only to those who had been with him during his public life and letting the church spread through their witness?

Perhaps the answer is to be found in the nature of salvation and the nature of the church. Salvation is not a matter of learning a new set of facts but of entering into a new relationship with God, a relationship through Jesus Christ. This new relationship in Christ involves being joined with Christ in his body, and this means being joined with others in the church. Accepting the gospel is not merely a matter of acknowledging that the good news about Jesus is true, but also a matter of being incorporated into the church.

The events of Pentecost day bear this out. In his sermon, Peter told about the life and crucifixion of Jesus, and asserted that "this Jesus God raised up, and of that all of us are witnesses" (Acts 2:32). Peter called upon the crowd to repent and be baptized in the name of Jesus Christ. Those that did became a part of a Christian community. They "devoted themselves to the apostles' teaching and fellowship, to the breaking of bread and the prayers. . . . All who believed were together and had all things in common" (2:42, 44).

The risen Jesus' plan was not simply to make sure that a great many people knew that he had triumphed over death but to invite them to be part of his new family. Jesus did not merely want to make the first-century evening news but to incorporate members into his body of followers. Jesus chose to have the good news spread by selected witnesses who could be the nucleus and leaders of the church.

A witness to Christ not only vouches for the truth of what Christ says but enters into a relationship with the one to whom she or he witnesses. A witness to Christ does not only say, "I have seen this," but also, "Join with me in accepting eternal life." The truth that a witness proclaims is not an abstract truth but a living truth, a truth by which the witness lives, a truth that witnesses can share with others only by sharing themselves.

5. CHRIST TO ONE ANOTHER

All this took place to fulfill what had been spoken by the Lord through the prophet:
 "Look, the virgin shall conceive and bear a son,
  and they shall name him Emmanuel,"
which means "God is with us."
—Matthew 1:22-23

Loneliness is a pervading affliction in modern times. Our technological society is not conducive to permanent relationships; mobility and freedom entail an inevitable amount of instability. Our grandparents may have lived most of their lives in one city or even in one neighborhood; our children can look forward to periodic moves and no permanent home.

Their best friend in school last year may have moved across the country during the summer.

The result of such impermanence and rootlessness is a feeling of loneliness. Family life becomes the last bastion of belonging, the last retreat where we can rely on being loved. But even family life lacks ultimate permanence. Children grow up and move away; parents become old and die.

God's answer to our deepest longing for love is Jesus Christ. Jesus is Emmanuel, a Hebrew name that means "God is with us." God is not aloof and unknowable; God bridged the distance between himself and us by becoming human in Jesus of Nazareth. In response to our loneliness, Jesus promises, "I am with you always, to the end of the age" (Matthew 28:20).

Paradoxically, in order for Jesus to remain with us, it was necessary for him to return to his Father: "It is to your advantage that I go away, for if I do not go away, the Advocate will not come to you; but if I go, I will send him to you" (John 16:7). Jesus is present to us now through his Holy Spirit. We can apply the same name to the Spirit that was applied to Jesus: Emmanuel, "God is with us."

Despite the pressures of modern society, despite the separations that inevitably come with time, we do not need to succumb to anxiety or loneliness. We have not been left orphans (John 14:18); we have been incorporated into the family of Jesus (Mark 3:33-35), made children of the Father by the Holy Spirit (Romans 8:14-16). In Christ we find stability; to Christ we belong; with Christ we have a permanent home.

Jesus promises that "where two or three are gathered in my name, I am there among them" (Matthew 18:20). The obvious sense of Jesus' words is a promise of his presence when we gather together in prayer. But there is another dimension of meaning to his words.

Paul taught that "as many of you as were baptized into Christ have clothed yourselves with Christ" (Galatians 3:27)—have "put on Christ" in some translations. No longer do we live just as ourselves, but we live in Christ. When we gather together in the name of Jesus, we do not merely gather as human beings coming into contact with one another. We gather as individuals who by the power of the Spirit have become incorporated into Christ and who manifest the presence of Christ in the world today. We gather to be the presence of Christ to each other.

Jesus wishes to heal the loneliness of others not only by the presence of his Holy Spirit, but also through our Spirit-filled presence. He wishes to manifest his love for others through our love for them. He wishes to bring a sense of permanence and stability to their lives not only through his steadfast reliability but also through our concrete acts of love and concern. The bonds of Christian fellowship we form with others are to be a sign and an aspect of Jesus' bond with them.

God is with us through the presence of the Holy Spirit. God is also with us through our loving presence to each other. We are called to imitate Christ even in his being Emmanuel: God is with us, through us.

6. BROTHERS AND SISTERS IN THE LORD

By contrast, the fruit of the Spirit is love, joy, peace, patience, kindness, generosity, faithfulness, gentleness, and self-control.
—Galatians 5:22

Paul's list of the fruits of the Spirit is a good summary of the character traits we all want to have. Instead of being worried and anxious, we would like to have a constant sense of peace. Instead of being sad or depressed, we would like to be filled with joy. Instead of being short tempered and irritable, we wish we were patient and gentle. We would like to have complete self-control, so that we won't do things that we shouldn't do.

We view the fruits of the Spirit as qualities that we hope to possess, qualities we will have when the sin in our lives has been eliminated and we are completely filled with the Holy Spirit.

There is another way of viewing the fruits of the Spirit, however—as characteristics of our relationships with one another. The fruits of the Spirit can be understood as flourishing *between* us, as brothers and sisters in the Lord, as well as *within* us, as individual Christians.

Paul lists love as the first fruit of the Spirit; elsewhere he provides a description of the love that the Spirit gives us: "Love is patient; love is kind; love is not envious or boastful or arrogant or rude. It does not insist on its own way; it is not irritable or resentful; it does not rejoice in wrongdoing, but rejoices in the truth. It bears all things, believes all things, hopes all things, endures all things" (1 Corinthians 13:4-7).

Most of these marks of love are descriptions of how we should relate to others. When we love others in the power of the Spirit, we are always ready to see their point of view and to trust them; we are willing to put their good above our own; we are ready to excuse and forgive mistakes they make. When we love others in the power of the Spirit, we will not be envious of their good fortune, even if we are experiencing difficult times ourselves. When we are moved by love, we neither resent the successes of our friends nor gloat over their failures.

On the other hand, when we are motivated by the worst in us, the result is the poisonous fruit of "enmities, strife, jealousy, anger, quarrels, dissensions, factions, envy" (Galatians 5:20-21). These weaknesses "of the flesh" destroy the unity that should exist between brothers and sisters in Christ. Enmities and strife, dissensions and factions splinter the body of Christ; jealousy and anger, quarrels and envy break the bond we have with each other in the Spirit.

Thus, just as the fruit of the Spirit is behavior that furthers our unity with one another, the fruit of self-indulgence is behavior that shatters this unity.

If we view the fruits of the Spirit as bonds between us instead of qualities we have inside ourselves, then we will try to grow in the fruits of the Spirit in a slightly different way. Our focus will no longer be narrowly upon ourselves but upon others and our relationships with them. Our concern will be less with a spiritual self-help program for ourselves than with the good of others and our service to them. We will pay less attention to ourselves and our own spiritual condition and more attention to others, striving to meet their needs and love them with the sacrificial love of Christ. And we will find that the more our focus is upon self-sacrificial service of others, the better our own spiritual condition will be. The fruits of the Spirit grow in the soil of love.

QUESTIONS FOR REFLECTION

1. What does it mean to you that you are a daughter or son of God? Do you find it natural to pray to God as your Father? What has God done to demonstrate to you that you are his beloved child?

2. If you were asked why you are a Christian, how would you answer? Is the way you live an invitation to others to embrace Jesus and become part of his family? How have

you most vividly experienced God's love for you through the loving acts of a brother or sister in Christ?

3. When have you been the most lonely? How have you experienced that "God is with us"? How have you been able to manifest God's presence to others?

4. If Paul's list of the fruits of the Spirit (Galatians 5:22) is a checklist for how you are to behave, how are you doing? What single thing might you do today to grow in one of the fruits of the Spirit?

PART FIVE

TO LOVE ONE ANOTHER

I. INDISCRIMINATE LOVE

[Jesus said:] "You have heard that it was said, 'You shall love your neighbor and hate your enemy.' But I say to you, Love your enemies and pray for those who persecute you, so that you may be children of your Father in heaven; for he makes his sun rise on the evil and on the good, and sends rain on the righteous and on the unrighteous. For if you love those who love you, what reward do you have? Do not even the tax collectors do the same? And if you greet only your brothers and sisters, what more are you doing than others? Do not even the Gentiles do the same? Be perfect, therefore, as your heavenly Father is perfect."

—Matthew 5:43-48

God seems guilty of indiscriminate love. He doesn't differentiate between those who deserve to have the sun shine upon them and those who do not. If we were charged with God's responsibility, we would likely pass judgment on the worth of each person and be more discriminating in whose crops received rain and whose did not.

Had we been devout Jews at the time of Jesus, we also would have been scandalized that he associated with those we were taught to reject. "Why does your teacher eat with tax collectors and sinners?" And Jesus would have given us the same answer he gave the Pharisees: "Those who are well have no need of a physician, but those who are sick" (Matthew 9:11-12).

Underlying our attitude toward others is our deeply held belief that we ourselves must, in the final analysis, earn our own salvation. Raised in a society that is achievement oriented, we view salvation as one more goal that we need to achieve—and achieve by our own unstinting effort.

If we find ourselves falling short of earning our salvation (as we inevitably must), then we become prey to feelings of guilt and self-condemnation. We have a hard time believing that God loves us despite our failings and unworthiness. We persist in believing that we have to earn our Father's love instead of accepting it as a free gift.

We also have a hard time believing that God loves others as he does. We judge others as we judge ourselves, adding up their good points and bad points, strengths and weaknesses, usually with a keener eye to their failures than to their successes. Because we do not accept God's unconditional love for ourselves, we do not believe in his unconditional love for others. And consequently we do not extend our own unconditional love to them, either.

Yet that is the call of Jesus to us: not to love others because they deserve our love, but to love them in imitation of the Father. We are called to an indiscriminate love, to a love that does not distinguish between those who are worthy of our love and those who are not, between enemies who harass us and friends who treat us kindly. Our love is to be as impartial as the sun that rises on bad men and women as well as on good, as the rain that falls for the honest and dishonest alike. We are to love people not as deserving or undeserving, but simply as people.

Jesus would call us one step further. He would call us, in imitation of him, to make a special effort to love those who are the hardest to love, and who therefore need our love the most. A physician does not enjoy illness but associates with sick people precisely because they need to be healed. Similarly, those who would seem to deserve our love least actually need our love most, if we are to imitate him who loves us without reserve.

2. CHARISMATIC GIFTS

> Above all, maintain constant love for one another, for love covers a multitude of sins. Be hospitable to one another without complaining. Like good stewards of the manifold grace of God, serve one another with whatever gift each of you has received. Whoever speaks must do so as one speaking the very words of God; whoever serves must do so with the strength that God supplies, so that God may be glorified in all things through Jesus Christ.
>
> —1 Peter 4:8-11

When we think of the New Testament's teaching on charismatic gifts, we immediately think of what St. Paul wrote to the church at Corinth (1 Corinthians 12–14). We might even think that if there had not been a particularly charismatic church at Corinth that demanded Paul's attention and correction, the gifts of the Spirit might have gone unmentioned in the pages of the New Testament.

Such an impression is incorrect; the gifts of the Spirit were not merely the peculiar endowment of the Corinthians but the heritage of every early Christian community. Paul's first letter to Corinth may contain the most extended teaching on the charismatic gifts, but it is far from being the only New Testament text to teach about them.

The First Letter of Peter was written some years after Paul wrote to the Corinthians. It was addressed to Christians living in five provinces of Asia Minor (1 Peter 1:1), an area that covers much of modern-day Turkey. It was therefore not written to a specific local church (as Paul's letters to Corinth were), but to a variety of Christian communities scattered over a broad area. It exhorted the members of these communities to be diligent in their use of the gifts of the Spirit, succinctly touching on the very points that Paul expounded at greater length.

Peter exhorts his readers to "serve one another with whatever gift each of you has received"; he clearly means a grace or charismatic gift to be used in the service of others. He does not provide an exhaustive list of what these gifts might be; rather each individual is to discover how he or she is equipped to serve others, and each community is to call forth its members in service.

Even though some gifts of service may appear rather natural and ordinary in their operation, they nonetheless are gifts that come from God. Those who teach, exhort, or explain Scripture are to use their gifts as if their words come from God—not that they can claim God's authority for their opinions, but that their words must be faithful to God's message. Those who serve (a very broad category) are to rely on God's strength and are to work conscientiously as people empowered by God, however humble their service. The only other gift that Peter explicitly addresses is hospitality: welcoming guests and providing them with lodging and food. Clearly Peter, like Paul, conceives of the charismatic gifts as widely distributed and greatly varied, but all gifts of grace nonetheless.

Peter also echoes Paul in making love for one another the context of spiritual gifts, and this is the key to understanding them. Our gifts of service are ways that God empowers us to love one another. If we follow Paul's advice to "pursue love" (1 Corinthians 14:1), we will find it much easier to discover what our gifts are and how they are to be used. We will have the pleasant surprise of discovering that we are empowered to love by God's grace working through us, overcoming our limitations and giving us the ability to serve.

Charisms were not given only to the early church; the church in every age needs special gifts of God that equip it to carry out the mission of Jesus Christ on earth. Our gifts of service may change over the years as our life situations and opportunities to serve change. But we never get beyond our need for the power of the Spirit if we are to carry out the works of love.

3. THE BOND THAT UNITES US

> When any of you has a grievance against another, do you dare to take it to court before the unrighteous, instead of taking it before the saints? . . .
> In fact, to have lawsuits at all with one another is already a defeat for you. Why not rather be wronged? Why not rather be defrauded?
> —1 Corinthians 6:1, 7

Paul takes the church at Corinth to task for permitting one of its members to bring a civil lawsuit against another member. The matter should have been resolved within the confines of the Christian community. For a Christian, the norm should be not to have lawsuits at all, preferring to be wronged rather than to take legal action against a fellow Christian.

It is easy to nod agreement to Paul's advice and overlook how different our practices are today. How many of us, if we were injured, would hesitate to sue another person simply because that person was a Christian? If someone refused to pay us a large amount that they owed us, would we turn the matter over to our pastor—again, simply because our debtor was a fellow Christian?

Perhaps courts of law were different in Paul's time. The Christian community was certainly different: smaller, more tightly knit, apparently more committed. But do these differences make Paul's teaching completely without point today? Is there something we can still learn from Paul's approach?

Paul's words make sense only if those who follow Christ

are joined to one another in some real way. Paul's exhortation assumes that a bond exists among Christians, a bond at least as strong as the bonds that hold a family together.

If Paul had been writing not to a Christian community but to a family, we would have no problem accepting his solution as a reasonable one. We would agree that there is something scandalous about a son's taking a father to court to redress a wrong or a brother's suing a sister, even if they had a valid case. There is something horribly wrong about members of the same family settling their differences by lawsuits; it indicates a breakdown in the bonds that unite a family.

For Paul, those who have found eternal life in Jesus Christ have been joined together by bonds that are even stronger than blood kinship. Paul does not compare the church to a family; he prefers the even stronger analogy of the unity of the human body (1 Corinthians 12:12-27). Our relationship with Christ makes us members of one body, joined to one another as hand is joined to arm, as sinew to bone. Hence it would be as scandalous to go to court against a fellow Christian as it would be outrageous for the right hand to sue the left or for the ear to sue the nose.

Jesus likewise taught that the bonds between his followers were to be even stronger than the bonds of a family. A disciple is justified in leaving behind father and mother and children to follow Jesus (Matthew 10:37-38). Jesus' mother and brothers "are those who hear the word of God and do it" (Luke 8:21).

The ability to let ourselves be wronged goes hand in hand with a willingness to forgive "seventy-seven times" (Matthew 18:22). Most of us will never have occasion to take anyone to court, but all of us have many occasions in which we can practice forgiveness. Our attitude toward our brothers and sisters in Christ must be one of putting the bond that unites us ahead of our disagreements and preferring their good to our own because we belong to the same family, the same body, the same Lord—who continues to forgive us no matter how many times or how grievously we have sinned.

4. BE RECONCILED WITH ONE ANOTHER

> [Jesus said:] "But I say to you that if you are angry with a brother or sister, you will be liable to judgment; and if you insult a brother or sister, you will be liable to the council; and if you say, 'You fool,' you will be liable to the hell of fire. So when you are offering your gift at the altar, if you remember that your brother or sister has something against you, leave your gift there before the altar and go; first be reconciled to your brother or sister, and then come and offer your gift."
>
> —Matthew 5:22-24

The gospels were written to preserve a record of the lived faith of the apostolic church. Not every saying or deed of Jesus was set down in writing (John 20:30; 21:25). Rather, the gospel evangelists selected those teachings of Jesus that provided guidance for the ongoing life of the church. The teachings of Jesus that deal with relationships should be understood as instructions for how Christians should relate to one another within the church.

The teachings of Jesus place a great stress upon unity among his followers. At the Last Supper Jesus prayed for his disciples, "that they may all be one. As you, Father, are in me and I am in you, may they also be in us, so that the world may believe that you have sent me" (John 17:21). Their unity was to be so profound that it would be a sign authenticating Jesus' mission from the Father.

Jesus not only prayed for unity among his disciples, but he instructed them about how their unity was to be preserved. He told them—and he tells us—that there must be no limit to forgiveness: "not seven times, but, I tell you, seventy-seven times" must we forgive a brother or sister who wrongs us (Matthew 18:22). We are to be slow in judging others, paying much more attention to the log in our own eye than to the speck in a fellow Christian's eye (7:1-5).

It is all too easy to let seeds of division grow in our midst. We can notice that others do not live out their faith in exactly the same way we do and feel that they are somehow less committed than we are. We can mistrust those we are not in steady contact with, simply because we don't understand the reasons for their actions. But Jesus' words to us are as plain as they were to John: "John answered, 'Master, we saw someone casting out demons in your name, and we tried to stop him, because he does not follow with us.' But Jesus said to him, 'Do not stop him; for whoever is not against you is for you'" (Luke 9:49-50).

If we are aware of a conflict with another, we must interrupt even the important duty of worship and act to bring about unity again. Jesus seems to make others the judges of our actions: if someone has something against us, it is up to us to take the first step to be reconciled.

The unity of the church is something for which we are all responsible. If the words of Jesus are to make a difference in our lives, they must guide us in our relationships with each other, warning us of the peril of disunity, commanding us to repair disunity whenever it occurs.

5. AS WE FORGIVE THOSE . . .

[Jesus said:] "The kingdom of heaven may be compared to a king who wished to settle accounts with his slaves. When he began the reckoning, one who owed him ten thousand talents was brought to him; and, as he could not pay, his lord ordered him to be sold, together with his wife and children and all his possessions, and payment to be made. So the slave fell on his knees before him, saying, 'Have patience with me and I will pay you everything.' And out of pity for him, the lord of that slave released him and forgave him the debt. But that same slave, as he went out, came upon one of his fellow slaves who owed him a hundred denarii; and seizing him by the throat, he said, 'Pay what you owe.' Then his fellow slave fell down and pleaded with him, 'Have patience with me, and I will pay you.' But he refused; then he went and threw him into prison until he would pay the debt. When his fellow slaves saw what had happened, they were greatly distressed, and they went and reported to their lord all that had taken place. Then his lord summoned him and said to him, 'You wicked slave! I forgave you all that debt because you pleaded with me. Should you not have had mercy on your fellow slave, as I had mercy on you?' And in anger his lord handed him over to be tortured until he would pay his entire debt. So my heavenly Father will also do to every one of you, if you do not forgive your brother or sister from your heart."

—Matthew 18:23-35

We might miss the full impact of this parable if we do not have some idea of how much a talent and a denarius were worth in the time of Jesus. If we take the amounts in this parable literally, the contrast between the two debts is staggering.

A denarius was the amount an ordinary worker earned in a day. The second slave (servant in some translations) owed the first slave about a hundred days' wages—not an insignificant amount, but a debt that could have been repaid over time. The first slave owed his master ten thousand talents. A talent was a weight of precious metal and by some calculations was equivalent to about six thousand denarii; this would mean that the first slave owed roughly sixty million days' wages. If the first slave were to work off his debt as an ordinary wage earner, it would have taken him around two hundred thousand years to repay it. This was clearly an impossibility, so his master forgave him the debt when he begged for mercy.

There was also a symbolic meaning to the debt of ten thousand talents. Ten thousand was the largest number in the Jewish numbering system, and a talent was the largest monetary value. Hence a debt of ten thousand talents was the largest conceivable debt. That, taught Jesus, is what our debt of sin to God is like. It is absolutely impossible for us to earn our way to heaven, no matter how hard and how long we work. Our debt is so huge that the only solution is for it to be forgiven. And God does that when we ask him to.

But God's forgiveness of us has implications for our forgiveness of each other. We will never be able to forgive as much as we have been forgiven, but we must forgive without limits. Peter asked, "Lord, if another member of the church sins against me, how often should I forgive? As many as seven times?" Jesus answered, "Not seven times, but, I tell you, seventy-seven times" (Matthew 18:21-22; some manuscripts of Matthew's gospel read, "seventy times seven times"). This was a vivid way for Jesus to say that there can't be any limits to our forgiveness.

We usually find it easiest to forgive others when they barely need our forgiveness. It is easier to forgive spilling milk on an old tablecloth than paint on a new rug. It is hardest to forgive wrongs that we suspect were deliberately done to us. But the standard of forgiveness that God has set does not allow us to discriminate among degrees of severity or to withhold our forgiveness for serious wrongs. We have been forgiven an immeasurably large debt; therefore no debt can ever be so large that we are excused from forgiving it ourselves.

Nor are we allowed to forgive grudgingly: Jesus told his disciples that they must forgive "from your heart" or risk jeopardizing their own forgiveness. Our call is to be children of our Father in heaven, who "makes his sun rise on the evil and on the good, and sends rain on the righteous and on the unrighteous" (Matthew 5:45). In forgiving each other, therefore, we must "be perfect, therefore, as your heavenly Father is perfect" (5:48). We must forgive others as we have been forgiven ourselves—as indeed we pray: "Forgive our trespasses, as we forgive those who trespass against us."

6. CASE STUDY: JONAH, GOD, AND NINEVEH

Now the word of the LORD came to Jonah son of Amittai, saying, "Go at once to Nineveh, that great city, and cry out against it; for their wickedness has come up before me." But Jonah set out to flee to Tarshish from the presence of the LORD.

—Jonah 1:1-3

Jonah is sometimes remembered only for having been in the belly of the fish for three days, which almost makes the fish the central character of the story. Yet the Book of Jonah contains an important message about God's plan of salvation.

The Book of Jonah is short (only 48 verses), and its story is simple. God wished to send Jonah to Nineveh with his word. Nineveh was the capital of the Assyrian empire, a hated enemy of Israel that had conquered the northern kingdom in 721 B.C. and deported many Israelites. Jonah fled at the prospect of taking God's message to the enemies of Israel. But a storm at sea and a great fish brought Jonah back, and God ordered him a second time to go to Nineveh.

Jonah obeyed this time and delivered God's message of judgment: "Forty days more, and Nineveh shall be overthrown!" (Jonah 3:4). But to Jonah's amazement, the inhabitants of Nineveh repented in sackcloth and ashes and God forgave them. This made Jonah indignant. He didn't want God to be a gracious God, "merciful, slow to anger, and abounding in steadfast love, and ready to relent from punishing" (4:2); Jonah had been looking forward to Nineveh's destruction. But God defended his mercy: "Should I not be concerned about Nineveh?" (4:11).

The Book of Jonah addresses a narrow nationalism that tempted God's people after the exile. Those who returned placed great emphasis on restoring the worship of God in all its purity. The laws of the covenant were enforced again, and foreign-born wives were sent away. While these measures were taken to restore religious and communal life, they had an unfortunate side effect: the Israelites were in danger of becoming blind to the larger dimensions of God's love and mercy. Israel was in danger of viewing itself as the only people God loved.

The Book of Jonah was written to correct this narrowness of vision. God's word came to the Israelite Jonah, but he did everything he could to evade God's mission for him. In contrast, God's word came to Nineveh—the pagan city—and the people immediately repented in sackcloth! Jonah was upset that God showed the people of Nineveh mercy: weren't they the enemy? But God defended his compassion and mercy and the universality of his love.

We also may need to be reminded of the breadth of God's love and the far-reaching intent of his plan. To the very extent that God has blessed us and called us to serve him, we can succumb to a narrowness of vision. We can become protective of what God has called us to do or be part of, particularly if we have to struggle to accomplish it or if we have to defend it against attacks or misunderstanding. As a result, we may be blind to the other ways God is acting to accomplish his purposes in the world today. In our effort to be faithful to what he has called us to do, we can be less sensitive to the different ways that he has chosen to work in others.

The book of Jonah can be a reminder that God's plan is always greater than our understanding, and God's love, always beyond our comprehension. Jonah is a warning against letting a narrowness of vision infect us. It can also be an encouragement to us: God is indeed a God of mercy and compassion, concerned about even those who are so clueless that they "do not know their right hand from their left" (Jonah 4:11).

QUESTIONS FOR REFLECTION

1. Have you ever thought that God was too tolerant of evildoers and indiscriminate in his love? What kind of people do you find it hardest to love? How might you find in the example of Jesus the inspiration to be more loving?

2. How have you experienced the Holy Spirit giving you the strength to love? What particular abilities did the Spirit give you to equip you to serve? How completely are you making use of your abilities now?

3. How much of a bond do you feel with other Christians simply because they are Christians? Is there a broken personal relationship that you need to take steps to repair? Is

there someone you need to forgive, even if the harm they did you seems unforgivable?

4. Have you ever tried to flee from what God was asking you to do? Were you any more successful than Jonah? How does the fact that God is merciful and loving give you hope? What task are you given because God is merciful and loving?

PART SIX

THE IMPORTANCE OF PRAYER

I. PLACING OUR TRUST IN GOD

[Jesus said:] "So I say to you, Ask, and it will be given you; search, and you will find; knock, and the door will be opened for you. For everyone who asks receives, and everyone who searches finds, and for everyone who knocks, the door will be opened. Is there anyone among you who, if your child asks for a fish, will give a snake instead of a fish? Or if the child asks for an egg, will give a scorpion? If you then, who are evil, know how to give good gifts to your children, how much more will the heavenly Father give the Holy Spirit to those who ask him!"

—Luke 11:9-13

Our ultimate search in life is our search for God. We may become distracted by many things along the way, but none of these distractions can substitute for our finding the one who made us and to whom we are called. Augustine wrote, "Our hearts are restless until they rest in you." Our hearts have been touched by God, and they are eager to discover more of God and encounter him more intimately. Each new revelation of God is but a prelude for the next; each taste of the goodness of God only increases our hunger for more.

Jesus' words to his disciples about asking, searching, and knocking apply to our own search for God and for his blessings. Jesus promised that the Father would send the Holy Spirit to those who asked, and it is the Spirit in us who is God's encounter with us. It is through the Spirit that God is revealed to us; it is through the gift of the Holy Spirit that God fulfills our search for him.

The examples Jesus chose vividly illustrate the trustworthiness of God in answering our prayers. Implicit in the examples is the premise that, as the perfect parent, God will provide for us better than even the best human parents could ever care for their children. On the most basic level, the examples show that God will always give us the nourishment we need.

The examples also reassure us that our heavenly Father will never deceive us. There is a deceptive similarity to the items Jesus contrasts in each of the pairs. By a snake, Jesus likely meant what we call an eel. The Law of Moses prohibited eating eels (Leviticus 11:9-12), so they were not acceptable substitutes for fish. There was a light-skinned type of scorpion that could be mistaken for a small egg when it rested in a curled position with its legs and tail tucked in. It would be a deadly "egg" to give to a child!

Normal parents, whatever their failings, would never refuse to provide food for their children when they needed it. Still less would they play cruel and dangerous tricks on their children in response to their requests: no inedible eels for fish or scorpions for eggs. And, Jesus taught, still less would our Father in heaven turn down our prayers or answer them in a cruelly deceptive way.

Jesus' characterization of his Father should reassure us that the Holy Spirit is indeed at work in our lives if we just ask for him. Most of us experience doubt or temptations to doubt at some point, particularly when it comes to our most intimate relationship with God. Did I experience something of the presence of God in prayer yesterday, or was it just my imagination? Did the Holy Spirit guide me as I spoke with a friend about Jesus last week, or were the words strictly my own? Was it the Spirit who moved me to stay up late interceding for peace in the world today, or was it my guilt at not doing anything to advance the cause of peace? Does God acknowledge my yearning for him? Is God drawing me to himself? We need to have discernment in judging what seem to be the promptings of the Spirit, but it is corrosive to our Christian life to doubt that the Spirit ever prompts us.

Jesus tells us, Seek my Father and you will find him; ask to receive my life and you will receive it; pray to be filled with the Holy Spirit and you will be filled. Your Father will not turn a deaf ear to your seeking and asking; nor will he give you counterfeit life or a misleading illusion of answered prayer. If you would neither deceive your children nor refuse to feed them, how much more can you rely on your Father in heaven to truly send you the Holy Spirit when you ask.

2. FINDING TIME TO PRAY

In the morning, while it was still very dark, [Jesus] got up and went out to a deserted place, and there he prayed. And Simon and his companions hunted for him. When they found him they said to him, "Everyone is searching for you."

—Mark 1:35-37

It can scarcely surprise us that Jesus prayed. What is striking, however, is the difficulty Jesus had in finding the time and solitude to pray, and the determination he showed in overcoming this difficulty.

Jesus attracted crowds wherever he went. On one occasion the crowds were too thick to bring a man on a stretcher to Jesus, so he had to be lowered through a hole in the roof (Mark 2:1-4). At other times the crowds kept Jesus from having any time to himself: "Then he went home; and the crowd came together again, so that they could not even eat" (3:19-20).

When Jesus and the disciples wished to be alone, their only alternative was to try to steal away—a tactic that didn't always work: "He said to them, 'Come away to a deserted place all by yourselves and rest a while.' For many were coming and going, and they had no leisure even to eat. And they went away in the boat to a deserted place by themselves. Now many saw them going and recognized them, and they hurried there on foot from all the towns and arrived ahead of them" (Mark 6:31-33).

Such a lifestyle hardly seems conducive to prayer. Our image of a life oriented to prayer is one of an unhurried pace, a regular schedule, silence, and of course, solitude. In contrast, the life of Jesus was akin to that of a presidential candidate: always in the public eye, never far from the clamor of the crowds, continually traveling from one place to another. Once when Jesus tried to avoid the crowds, a scribe came up to him and said, "Teacher, I will follow you wherever you go." Jesus' reply to him was that "Foxes have holes, and birds of the air have nests; but the Son of Man has nowhere to lay his head" (Matthew 8:18-20).

Yet Jesus did spend time in prayer. Sometimes he would send the disciples on ahead, while he would go up into the hills to pray (Mark 6:45-46). Sometimes he arose early in the morning (1:35); sometimes he stayed up late, praying far into the night (6:48). And sometimes he managed to steal away, despite the presence of the crowd: "Many crowds would gather to hear him and to be cured of their diseases. But he would withdraw to deserted places and pray" (Luke 5:15-16).

We can learn the way of prayer from Jesus and draw encouragement from his life of prayer. If we must contend with erratic schedules and the demands of family life, so too did Jesus contend with the demands of those who came to him for instruction and healing. If the pace of modern life seems too rapid to allow us the luxury of prayer, the public ministry of Jesus was no less hectic. If we have trouble finding a quiet place alone with God, Jesus experienced the same difficulty. If our job demands a lot of us, Jesus' ministry demanded far more of him.

The example of Jesus teaches us that we need frequent times of communion with his Father. It also teaches us that we may have to overcome obstacles in order to have this time. The ideal would be for us to have a regular time for prayer in our daily schedule. In reality, we may have to make time as best we can each day. The tenacity with which Jesus made time for his prayer should be our model. We should keep in mind his determination to pray as we set out to create a prayer time for ourselves.

The example of Jesus is also reassuring. We may feel guilty because our prayer time is irregular, because our day is fragmented by hundreds of demands, because our solitude is constantly invaded. Jesus knows that we are not twelfth-century nuns or monks. He will understand our failures, as long as we try to make time for prayer with the same determination he had in finding time to be with his Father.

3. INTERCESSION

> We know love by this, that he laid down his life for us—and we ought to lay down our lives for one another.
>
> —1 John 3:16

None of us is able to lay down our life in the measure that Jesus gave his life for us. Yet all of us are called to a love for one another that knows no limits, a love that would accept even death itself should that be asked of us.

To love others as Jesus loves them is a lofty call. It is also a call that can get obscured by the daily routine of our lives, by the complexities of modern society, by the ambiguities of the situations in which we find ourselves. Even if the Holy Spirit has implanted in us a burning desire to love without reserve, translating that desire into effective action can some-times prove difficult.

The more united in love we become with others, the more we become aware of their needs. The more we accept others into our lives as brothers and sisters in the Lord, the more we become aware of the areas of hurt in their lives. And as we grow in our love for one another, we become increasingly aware of how much more we are called to love.

Sometimes the needs of others can be met rather simply. We can make an extra effort to befriend the lonely and offer encouragement to the insecure; we can visit the sick and bring meals to the homebound. But sometimes the needs of oth-ers are beyond our ability to satisfy and their hurts beyond our ability to heal. We cannot guarantee a safe delivery to a mother experiencing a difficult pregnancy; we cannot fill the void left in a child's life by the untimely death of a parent. We sometimes watch helplessly as a marriage breaks up, or as older children reject the love and faith of their parents.

Yet as Christians we are equipped with an ability to love that goes beyond our own limitations: we are authorized to turn to our Father with our concerns for others. Our love need not be limited by our own capabilities; our love can be expressed in prayer.

Intercession is not a substitute for expressing our love in effective action. But neither should intercession be a last resort—something we only have recourse to when all else fails. Rather, intercessory prayer should be a dimension of our con-cern for others and accompany all our attempts to meet their needs. The more intensely we love others, the more aware we should be of the limitations of our love. As we experience the love of God for us, we should increasingly realize how much more God loves others than we are able to love.

We know that God welcomes our prayers and hears them;

we know that prayer does make a difference. Through love we are drawn to pray for each other, as an indispensable dimension of our love.

To persevere in daily prayer for others can be truly a laying down of our lives for them. There may be times when we are attracted to intercessory prayer and find it a joy. There may also be times when it loses its appeal and we are tempted to neglect it. Our faithfulness in daily intercession for the needs of others requires that we put them first, ahead of our comfort or convenience. With steadfast intercession we must "bear one another's burdens" and so "fulfill the law of Christ" (Galatians 6:2).

4. PRAYER AND PERSISTENCE

> Jesus left that place and went away to the district of Tyre and Sidon. Just then a Canaanite woman from that region came out and started shouting, "Have mercy on me, Lord, Son of David; my daughter is tormented by a demon." But he did not answer her at all. And his disciples came and urged him, saying, "Send her away, for she keeps shouting after us." He answered, "I was sent only to the lost sheep of the house of Israel." But she came and knelt before him, saying, "Lord, help me." He answered, "It is not fair to take the children's food and throw it to the dogs." She said, "Yes, Lord, yet even the dogs eat the crumbs that fall from their masters' table." Then Jesus answered her, "Woman, great is your faith! Let it be done for you as you wish." And her daughter was healed instantly.
>
> —Matthew 15:21-28

A troubling incident. Jesus first ignores this woman and then insults her, comparing her to a dog. He exhibits no compassion for the woman or her daughter, nor any inclination to counteract the work of demons. Instead Jesus takes a narrow view of the scope of his mission. It is as if a paramedic refused to help a seriously injured woman because she came from the wrong neighborhood.

Despite these troublesome elements, we can interpret this incident as a parable about prayer and about our relationship with God, and draw some lessons from it.

Jesus' first response to the woman's request was silence: "He did not answer her at all." Similarly, God sometimes seems silent and unresponsive to our prayers. We wonder why it is so, just as this woman must have wondered why the man she acknowledged as Lord ignored her. There is no simple answer to our bewilderment, but there are precedents.

The disciples' request that Jesus "send her away" might have meant, "heal her daughter so that she will stop pestering us." They would then have been adding their plea to that of the woman. Sometimes it might seem to us that the prayers of our friends on our behalf are in vain. We wonder if we are somehow excluded from those whom God loves and cares for; we wonder what is wrong with us if even the prayers of others for us seem ineffective.

Jesus rebuffed this woman with a theological obstacle: he was sent only to the Jewish people. But this did not stop her. She did not argue with Jesus; she simply knelt at his feet, acknowledged him as her Lord, and begged him to help her. How could he refuse such a humble and persistent plea? But he did, and with an insult. To be compared to a scavenging dog must have seemed a slap in the face to her. Have any of us ever been so rebuffed by God?

Yet she continued her pleading. Neither the silence of Jesus nor his denial made her waver. How much she must have loved her afflicted daughter! She was determined that her daughter be healed, no matter the cost to herself. So she humbled herself even further, accepting Jesus' insult and making it a part

YOUR WORD SPEAKS TO ME

of her prayer. If the New Testament provides us with a living example of the "need to pray always and not to lose heart" (Luke 18:1), it is surely Jesus' encounter with this woman.

And Jesus responds! We cannot imagine that he had been playacting or merely testing the woman up to this point. It seems more likely that her humble persistence won him over. But note that he does not say to her, "Woman, you have great persistence," or, "Woman, you are truly a nag." He says, "Woman, great is your faith." What was her faith? Not merely that Jesus could heal her daughter; she believed that from the very first. The faith that won Jesus over seems rather to have been her unshakable belief that he would hear her prayer, despite his silence, despite theological barriers, despite a direct rebuff. She refused to take no for an answer.

This almost seems a dangerous faith: shouldn't we accept a no from God as his will for us? But Jesus responded to such faith and commended it. He would thereby seem to invite our own persistence, even stubbornness, in prayer.

Even as a parable about prayer, however, this passage has its perplexing elements. It doesn't give us simple answers so much as an encounter to reflect on, as we try to grow in prayer and in understanding of our own relationship with God.

5. JESUS' PRAYER, OUR PRAYER

[Jesus] came out and went, as was his custom, to the Mount of Olives; and the disciples followed him. When he reached the place, he said to them, "Pray that you may not come into the time of trial." Then he withdrew from them about a stone's throw, knelt down, and prayed, "Father, if you are willing, remove this cup from me; yet, not my will but yours be done." Then an angel from heaven appeared to him and gave him strength. In his anguish he prayed more earnestly,

106

> and his sweat became like great drops of blood falling down on the ground.
>
> —Luke 22:39-44

Jesus' agony in the garden is one of the events of his life that demands our reverent and silent gaze at its unfathomable mystery. We can join with Jesus in celebrating the wedding feast at Cana, sharing his joy and the joy of the newly married couple. We can trudge with Jesus along the back roads of Galilee, even when the days are long and hot and the evenings' lodgings uncertain. We can even, like Thomas, decide, "Let us also go, that we may die with him" (John 11:16) when the cross looms ahead. But at the agony in the garden we must draw back. The scene overwhelms us, as a Son in agony confronts his Father's will for him, as a man prostrates himself before God in wrenching surrender of his life. There was good reason why Jesus left his friends behind, going a stone's throw farther before beginning his prayer.

Yet the agony in the garden, like every incident in the gospels, demands our reflection and has its particular message for us. As we read how Matthew, Mark, and Luke describe it, we are struck by the fact that it was a real agony, not merely a pious pretense. Jesus was "distressed and agitated . . . grieved, even to death. . . . He threw himself on the ground" (Mark 14:33-35). Yet even in his distress, he prayed to God as his "Abba, Father" (14:36), asking him to "remove this cup from me; yet, not my will but yours be done" (Luke 22:42). John in his gospel's counterpart to the agony in the garden has Jesus admit, "Now my soul is troubled," but quickly jumps to the conclusion of his prayer: "And what should I say—'Father, save me from this hour'? No, it is for this reason that I have come to this hour. Father, glorify your name" (John 12:27-28).

These glimpses of Jesus' prayer to his Father as he faced what he must have known would be an agonizing death give us much to ponder as we contemplate the mystery of God become man. But they also give us a glimpse of the depths of meaning of the words we say when we pray the Our Father. The prayer Jesus taught his followers mirrors his own prayer in the garden and takes on its greatest meaning as our participation in his prayer to his Father.

"Pray then in this way: Our Father in heaven, hallowed be your name. Your kingdom come, your will be done" (Matthew 6:9-10). The echo of his prayer is unmistakable: "Abba, Father. . . . Glorify your name. . . . Not my will but yours be done." The words we often say so mechanically, so unthinkingly, so lightly, were the words that Jesus prayed in anguish, as his sweat fell to the ground like great drops of blood. If only we realized what we were praying! If only we realized the cost to Jesus in praying this prayer!

Even his injunction to his friends, "Pray that you may not come into the time of trial" has its echo in the Our Father. Matthew's version of the prayer that Jesus taught us reads, "And do not bring us to the time of trial, but rescue us from the evil one" (Matthew 6:13)—a petition we pray as, "and lead us not into temptation but deliver us from evil."

No doubt there are other parallels between the prayer that Jesus taught us and the prayers of Jesus recorded in the gospels. But the correspondence between the prayer of Jesus on the eve of his death and the prayer that we say as his followers is too striking to be a matter of mere coincidence. It is an invitation to us to reflect deeply on that moment when Jesus offered himself to his Father in complete confidence, yet with undeniable human agony. It is an invitation to offer ourselves to our Father, despite the price such offering demands of us. It is a reminder that our Father asks us to give ourselves over to his will and his glory no less completely than Jesus gave himself. It is a warning to never say lightly those words that cost Jesus so much. And it is finally the joyous assurance that because of Jesus we have a way to our Father, our Abba in heaven, our God who loves us enough to adopt us as his children.

QUESTIONS FOR REFLECTION

1. What is the most important instance in your life of God's answering your prayer? How absolute is your trust that God loves you with a greater love than you have ever received from another person or had for another person?

2. How regularly do you spend time in prayer? What are the greatest obstacles you face in having quality time for prayer? What can you learn from the example of Jesus?

3. For whom do you pray? How do you pray for them? How faithfully do you pray for them?

4. How do you react when God seems to ignore your prayers? How do you discern when to accept "no" as God's answer to your prayers and when to keep bombarding God with your pleas?

5. Which petitions of the Our Father have the most meaning for you? When have you found it easy to pray, "thy will be done"? When have you found it the most difficult to say to God, "your will, not mine, be done"?

PART SEVEN

MAINTAINING PERSPECTIVE

I. THE BASICS

> He has told you, O mortal, what is good;
>   and what does the LORD require of you
> but to do justice, and to love kindness,
>   and to walk humbly with your God?
>
> —Micah 6:8

Chapter 6 of Micah begins with God accusing his people, putting them on trial, and demanding to know how he has wronged them that they should treat him as they do (verses 1-5). God's people respond by wondering to themselves how they can placate God's anger (verses 6-7). They consider offering sacrifice. Perhaps a few choice year-old calves? No? Then maybe slaughtering a few thousand rams will please him. Or if that doesn't work, perhaps pouring out a torrent of valuable oil as a libation will buy his forgiveness. And if that doesn't do it, perhaps we could consider offering our firstborn children as a sacrifice for our sins.

God interrupts these deliberations to point out that he has already told his people what he requires of them. They do not need to wonder how many rams or gallons of oil it takes to make him happy. They certainly do not need to think about human sacrifice. What God asks of them is quite simple: "to do justice, and to love kindness, and to walk humbly with your God."

Scripture points out that a life pleasing to God is simpler than we might believe. When Jesus was asked, "What must I do to inherit eternal life?" he solicited the response, "You shall love the Lord your God with all your heart, and with all your soul, and with all your strength, and with all your mind; and your neighbor as yourself." Jesus then commented that one who did this would indeed have life (Luke 10:25-28). In

Matthew's presentation of this teaching, Jesus states that all else is based on these two commandments (Matthew 22:40).

These two commandments to love God and neighbor demand everything we have and all that we are. We need the other commandments to spell out what is contained in these two great commands. Yet it is striking that when Jesus was asked what was necessary for eternal life, he did not deliver the Sermon on the Mount. He rather drew attention to the basis of the Sermon on the Mount, the commands on which all else depends.

Likewise, when John was writing some years later to reaffirm the gospel against false teaching, he said simply, "This is his commandment, that we should believe in the name of his Son Jesus Christ and love one another, just as he has commanded us. All who obey his commandments abide in him, and he abides in them" (1 John 3:23-24). There is no long list of requirements, only a recitation of the basics.

A tragic flaw of some Pharisees was that they forgot the basics in their zeal to obey the fine print of the law. Hence Jesus felt compelled to cry out, "Woe to you Pharisees! For you tithe mint and rue and herbs of all kinds, and neglect justice and the love of God; it is these you ought to have practiced, without neglecting the others" (Luke 11:42). To give a tenth of garden spices as if they were a major crop but to ignore God and act unjustly is surely to miss the mark.

It is easy for us too to miss the mark, to ignore the basics while getting bogged down in the details. We can be like Martha, who was so zealous to prepare a fine dinner for Jesus that she ignored him as her guest. Mary, who simply sat at his feet, earned his praise. "Martha, Martha, you are worried and distracted by many things; there is need of only one thing. Mary has chosen the better part, which will not be taken away from her" (Luke 10:41-42).

Mary saw that the most important way to welcome Jesus into her home was to pay attention to him. A fine dinner in his honor would undoubtedly have been appreciated, but not at the expense of ignoring him in favor of cooking it.

It is easy for us to be like Martha today. Our world is complex, and our lives are full of responsibilities. We want to do the right thing, but we get so distracted by the details that we forget why we are doing them and whom we want to serve. We need to be continually reminded of the basics: to do justice, to love kindness, to walk humbly with our God.

2. HEALING ON THE SABBATH

> [Jesus] entered the synagogue, and a man was there who had a withered hand. They watched him to see if he would cure him on the sabbath, so that they might accuse him. And he said to the man who had the withered hand, "Come forward." Then he said to them, "Is it lawful to do good or to do harm on the sabbath, to save life or to kill?" But they were silent. He looked around at them with anger; he was grieved at their hardness of heart and said to the man, "Stretch out your hand." He stretched it out, and his hand was restored. The Pharisees went out and immediately conspired with the Herodians against him, how to destroy him.
>
> —Mark 3:1-6

In our love for Jesus, we have a hard time imagining that anyone who met him could hate him. Yet the sad record of the gospels is that Jesus met obstinate opposition, even from some religious leaders, and this opposition led to his death.

What did Jesus do to arouse such antagonism? The gospels describe opposition to Jesus arising over his healing on the sabbath or otherwise not keeping the sabbath holy in the way his critics thought he should.

When Jesus healed the sick man by the pool in Jerusalem and told him to pick up his sleeping mat and walk, the reaction of Pharisees was to exclaim, "It is the sabbath; it is not lawful for you to carry your mat" (John 5:10). John notes that some began persecuting Jesus "because he was doing such things on the sabbath" (5:16).

When Jesus healed a man who was born blind, his opponents did everything they could to deny that a miracle had taken place—even questioning the man's parents to make sure that he had truly been blind (John 9:18-23). But despite the clear evidence that in Jesus the power of God had been made present in their midst, they continued to deny it: "This man is not from God, for he does not observe the sabbath" (John 9:16).

Perhaps the most ludicrous response to one of Jesus' miracles was the reaction of a synagogue official. Jesus had healed a woman who had been crippled for eighteen years, but it was the sabbath and the official feared that others might also come to him to be healed. So he told the crowd that gathered, "There are six days on which work ought to be done; come on those days and be cured, and not on the sabbath day" (Luke 13:14).

We must marvel at such blindness: to try to deny the manifest power of God at work in Jesus, to try to limit the days on which God was free to heal, and to want to do away with the one who was healing the afflicted but without complying with their rules.

What was the cause of such blindness? It stemmed in part from emphasizing obedience to the letter of the law and multiplying the details of the law. God did command, "Remember the sabbath day, and keep it holy" (Exodus 20:8), abstaining from work. But this law had become so filled with prescriptions of what did and did not constitute work, that even a healed man's picking up his bedroll or the disciples' picking grains of wheat as they walked through a field (Mark 2:23-24) were judged violations of the law. When Jesus didn't abide by these minute prescriptions, then his critics refused to see good in anything he did.

That was a real tragedy. Jesus didn't heal only on the Sabbath, he healed every day of the week. But because what he did one day a week did not conform to the Pharisees' rules for what was acceptable, they refused to accept what he did the other six days of the week. They blinded themselves to who Jesus was and set out to destroy him.

Does this tragedy have a lesson for us? Do we let our preconceived notions of how God ought to act limit our awareness of how or through whom he might be acting today? Do we presume that there is only one way of being pleasing to God—namely, our way? Do we insist that the pattern that works best for us must therefore be the pattern for everyone? And when others do not accept or live up to the full truth, do we blind ourselves to the truth they do live by, to the life of God that they do have?

What makes the rejection of Jesus by his opponents so doubly tragic was the fervor with which they did it. They were zealous to uphold the law as they understood it; they were sincere in their belief that no one who broke their regulations could be from God. But they were also so misguided and blind that in striving to serve God by obeying his law, they managed to reject God's own Son.

3. TWO PRAYERS

[Jesus] also told this parable to some who trusted in themselves that they were righteous and regarded others with contempt. "Two men went up to the temple to pray, one a Pharisee and the other a tax collector. The Pharisee, standing by himself, was praying thus, 'God, I thank you that I am not like other people: thieves, rogues, adulterers, or even like this tax collector. I fast twice a week; I give a tenth of all my income.' But the tax collector, standing far off, would not even look up to heaven, but was beating his breast and saying, 'God, be merciful to me, a sinner!' I tell you, this man went down to his home justified rather than the other."

—Luke 18:9-14

To understand this parable, we must take the prayers of the Pharisee and the tax collector at face value: we must assume that they meant what they prayed and were not putting on an act.

The prayer of the Pharisee conveys both his true devotion and a tragic flaw in his perspective. He fasted twice a week; he was scrupulous in paying tithes on his income. He was not engaged in a sinful occupation, like collecting taxes. He probably was not an unjust man; he didn't commit adultery. He gave thanks to God for his righteousness—after all, he came to the temple to pray. In contrast, a good deal of the rest of the world was unjust and adulterous; a good many other Jews were slipshod in their observance of the law. The prayer of the Pharisee contained much truth.

Yet it was not a prayer that met with God's favor. Despite the truth of all that the Pharisee said about himself, his basic attitude was tragically wrong. His virtue had become a source of pride; he despised anyone who could not live up to the code of conduct that he followed.

The prayer of the tax collector likewise rings true. He was engaged in what was, with good reason, considered a sinful occupation; he could not come up with an impressive list of religious accomplishments. He was aware that he fell short

117

of fulfilling the law at many points. He consequently felt very sinful and at a distance from God. He did not pray a prayer of thanks to God; he could only dare a humble prayer of reliance on God's mercy. But his prayer found favor in God's sight.

We can have characteristics of both the Pharisee and the tax collector when we pray. We are aware of the graces we have received from God; we are aware that we are leading lives that are virtuous when compared with the ways of the world. And we should be humbly grateful for everything that God has given us. But we can sometimes fall into viewing others through the Pharisee's eyes, subtly looking down on them because they haven't accomplished what we have or because they don't live the way that we do. Jesus' parable is a stark reminder that no matter how privileged or virtuous we are, and no matter how misguided or sinful other people may be, we earn God's displeasure by judging or despising others.

We can also find ourselves praying as the tax collector prayed, aware of how far we fall short of God's plan for us, feeling at a distance from God, unable to pray a prayer of thanksgiving or praise with any conviction. Yet God was pleased by the tax collector's humble prayer. God loved the tax collector in spite of his sinfulness, and he honored the tax collector's cry for mercy. God loves us and will likewise hear our prayers for mercy—no matter how unholy we feel, no matter how aware we are of our sins, no matter how distant we feel ourselves to be from God.

4. MARTHA AND MARY

He entered a certain village, where a woman named Martha welcomed him into her home. She had a sister named Mary, who sat at the Lord's feet and listened to what he was saying. But Martha

> was distracted by her many tasks; so she came to him and asked, "Lord, do you not care that my sister has left me to do all the work by myself? Tell her then to help me." But the Lord answered her, "Martha, Martha, you are worried and distracted by many things; there is need of only one thing. Mary has chosen the better part, which will not be taken away from her."
>
> —Luke 10:38-42

Martha and Mary, although sisters, were quite different from each other. Martha strikes us as the better organized, the harder working, the more dependable. It was Martha who made the meal and took care of arrangements when Jesus visited their home (see also John 12:1-2). We can easily picture the kind of woman Martha was—the kind who gets pressed into service today for church dinners.

Mary was quite different. She strikes us as oblivious to the practical side of life. She didn't pitch in to help Martha get dinner so that both of them could then have listened to Jesus; the thought may never have crossed her mind. When Lazarus died, it was left to Martha to curtail her grieving and welcome Jesus; Mary stayed in the house, wrapped up in her mourning (John 11:20). In John's gospel, Mary was the one who anointed Jesus with very costly ointment—ointment that could have been sold for "three hundred denarii" (John 12:5). When we realize that a denarius was the standard wage for a day's work (Matthew 20:1-16), the astonished protests at her action (Matthew 26:8; John 12:4) take on more meaning: this impractical woman had just poured out a year's wages—from a human point of view, a sheer waste!

Martha and Mary were indeed opposites—but Jesus loved them both. We might have expected him to show favoritism for hardworking, dependable Martha. But if anything, Jesus had a preference for unpredictable Mary. While Jesus clearly valued reliability and good judgment in his followers, he also defended Mary when she didn't quite come up to the mark. After all, it was a little thoughtless of her to leave Martha with all the work, and it was an outrageous extravagance to spend a year's wages on a gesture of the moment. Yet Jesus took Mary's part, judging her according to the love for him in her heart, rather than according to the usual standards of proper conduct.

This is not to say he loved Martha any the less. Rather the lesson for us might be that Jesus is capable of loving people who are quite different from each other. There is no one standard design or personality type that every Christian must strive to be. There is not even one best or most responsible way for every Christian to live. If there was, we would clearly think that it was Martha's way. Yet Jesus refused to criticize Mary for behaving quite differently from Martha. If there is one way, it is the way of love: a way manifested both by hardworking Martha and by carefree Mary.

5. CASE STUDY: THE EPHESIANS

"To the angel of the church in Ephesus write: . . .

"I know your works, your toil and your patient endurance. I know that you cannot tolerate evildoers; you have tested those who claim to be apostles but are not, and have found them to be false. I also know that you are enduring patiently and bearing up for the sake of my name, and that you have not grown weary. But I have this against you, that you have abandoned the love you had at first."

—Revelation 2:1, 2-4

Ephesus was not the easiest city in which to live a Christian life. It was one of the larger cities of the Roman Empire, a regional capital and trade center. The worship of pagan gods was particularly entrenched there. For a young church to take root and survive in Ephesus was in itself a testimony to the power of the Holy Spirit.

When Paul made his final pastoral visit to the leaders of the church at Ephesus, he warned them that after he was gone, "savage wolves will come in among you, not sparing the flock" (Acts 20:29). These wolves would be Christians who taught a distorted gospel: "Some even from your own group will come distorting the truth in order to entice the disciples to follow them. Therefore be alert" (20:30-31).

What happened after Paul uttered this warning, sometime near the middle of the first century? The Acts of the Apostles tells us nothing more, and little information can be drawn from the Letter to the Ephesians. However, the church in Ephesus is one of the seven churches addressed by name in the opening chapters of the Book of Revelation. Scholars debate the date that Revelation was written, but it was sometime around the end of the first century. Hence, its words to the church in Ephesus give us a glimpse of this church about fifty years after Paul proclaimed the gospel there.

The Ephesians apparently took Paul's words very much to heart and were zealous for orthodoxy. They are commended in Revelation for exposing false apostles and rejecting false teaching. Likewise, they are commended for persevering in their faith despite trials and persecutions. The Ephesians labored hard in the decades since Paul had brought them the gospel; they suffered much, and suffered it patiently. They held to the truth with tenacity, despite the attacks of false teachers from within and the pagan environment from without.

But after God's word in Revelation commends the Ephesians for their tenacity and orthodoxy, it takes them to task for losing the love that they once had. "But I have this against you, that you have abandoned the love you had at first" (2:4).

Was it their love of God or their love of each other that had cooled—or both? The text doesn't specify. But the text makes clear that this loss of love was a most serious matter: "Remember then from what you have fallen; repent, and do the works you did at first. If not, I will come to you and remove your lampstand from its place, unless you repent" (2:5).

What had gone wrong in Ephesus? Had their zeal for orthodoxy led to the rigidity and narrowness that Jesus found in the Pharisees: an attention to detail that lost sight of the larger picture, a vigilance for deviations from the truth that overshadowed love and mercy? Had their patient endurance of trials and suffering and persecution become a matter of joyless stoicism, a certain numbness to life that allowed them to survive everything but rejoice in nothing?

Clearly, vigilant orthodoxy and rugged endurance were necessary for the church's survival at Ephesus; the praise they received in Revelation was well warranted. But orthodoxy and endurance are not enough, particularly if they become the chief virtues of a community at the expense of love. Hence the word of God in Revelation called the Ephesians to return to their first love—to the joy in God's presence they once experienced, to the unconditional generosity toward each other that once marked their community.

QUESTIONS FOR REFLECTION

1. What is the most basic thing Jesus asks you to do as his follower? What most impedes you from loving God and loving your neighbor as you should? What could you do to remove this obstacle?

2. To what extent do you see something of yourself in the Pharisee in Jesus' parable of the Pharisee and the tax collector? To what extent do you see something of yourself in the tax collector?

3. Are you more like Martha or Mary? If you tend to be more like Martha, what can you learn from Mary? If you tend to be more like Mary, what can you learn from Martha?

4. How has the love you first experienced for God evolved over the years? Has your joy at being a child of God grown deeper or dried up? Has your love for others become more self-sacrificing?

PART EIGHT

THE STRENGTH TO PERSEVERE

I. THE TEMPTATION TO TURN BACK

> The whole congregation of the Israelites complained against Moses and Aaron in the wilderness. The Israelites said to them, "If only we had died by the hand of the LORD in the land of Egypt, when we sat by the fleshpots and ate our fill of bread; for you have brought us out into this wilderness to kill the whole assembly with hunger."
>
> —Exodus 16:2-3

Egypt was a land of bitter oppression for the descendants of Abraham. "The Israelites groaned under their slavery, and cried out. Out of the slavery their cry for help rose up to God" (Exodus 2:23). God heard their prayers and sent Moses to deliver them. Through Moses, God worked mighty signs, and the Israelites were delivered from Egypt. Their freedom came in the parting of the sea and the destruction of the Egyptian army. "Israel saw the great work that the LORD did against the Egyptians. So the people feared the LORD and believed in the LORD and in his servant Moses" (14:31), and they joined in singing a glorious song of victory to the Lord (15:1-21).

Their rejoicing and trust lasted all of three days once they were in the wilderness (Exodus 15:22). Then in their thirst they "complained against Moses, saying, 'What shall we drink?'" and the Lord provided water (15:24-25). Then they complained that they were hungry, and the Lord provided manna (16:1-36). Then they grumbled that they were tired of eating manna ("What are we having for breakfast today?" "Manna." "*Again?*") and longed to return to the fish and cucumbers and melons and onions of Egypt (Numbers 11:1-15). Their complaints repeatedly expressed their longing to return to Egypt: "'Would it not be better for us to go back to Egypt?' So they said to one another, 'Let us choose a captain and go back to Egypt'" (14:3-4).

The exodus of the Israelites out of Egypt and their time in the desert stand as a pattern of the Christian life. Jesus experienced glory on the mount of transfiguration—but also knew the agony of crucifixion on the mound of Golgotha. Paul knew the power of Christ in him, even to raising the dead back to life (Acts 20:10-12), but also suffered beatings, shipwreck, hunger, rejection, and imprisonment (2 Corinthians 11:23-29).

We may have been granted a glorious experience of God and a taste of his great love for us. And we may then, after a period of time, have found ourselves in the desert, beset by difficulties that we thought had been resolved long ago.

Egypt was oppression for the Israelites, and their deliverance from it was the most triumphant moment of their existence. Yet in the desert they were only conscious of their thirst and hunger and longed to return to their slavery. We may have been delivered from a life that was heading for death, and delivered in a way that charged us with enthusiasm for the kingdom of God. Yet in the midst of our present trials and hunger, our past life may look appealing once again. Like the Israelites, we may be tempted to turn back.

That we are so tempted should not surprise us. The experience of the Israelites has been set down in Scripture so that we may learn from it (1 Corinthians 10:6, 11). If, after their triumphal deliverance from oppression, they were tempted to turn back when trials came, we should not be surprised to be similarly tempted ourselves.

Scripture teaches us that the temptation to turn back must be resisted, no matter how dry the sand of the desert or how appealing the delights of Egypt. Scripture teaches that beyond the desert there is a land promised to us; beyond Good Friday there is Easter morning. Jesus attained resurrection because he did not turn back; he promises his resurrection to us, if we persevere in our journey with him.

2. MIDDAY

> For God is not unjust; he will not overlook your work and the love that you showed for his sake in serving the saints, as you still do. And we want each one of you to show the same diligence so as to realize the full assurance of hope to the very end, so that you may not become sluggish, but imitators of those who through faith and patience inherit the promises.
>
> —Hebrews 6:10-12

There comes a midday time to the lives of many dedicated Christians—a time when the initial enthusiasm of conversion or commitment is only a memory, a time when growth in the Christian life seems to be stalled, a time when everything seems to be sliding backward into dry mediocrity. The fire of first love has been quenched by time and trivia; the goal seems more distant than ever.

The writers of the New Testament knew about the temptations that come at the midday of the Christian life, and wrote words of encouragement to help us remain faithful despite difficulties. The Letter to the Hebrews takes a very down-to-earth approach. We may be able to look back upon times in which our commitment to God was uncomplicated and our service to his people was unstinting. We may still be giving ourselves in service, even if we no longer find it as fulfilling as we once did. The Letter to the Hebrews proclaims to us that God could hardly be so unjust as to overlook our love for him and all that we have done in his service. We are reminded of Jesus' words, "Whoever gives even a cup of cold water to one of these little ones in the name of a disciple—truly I tell you, none of these will lose their reward" (Matthew 10:42). We need to acknowledge that this promise also applies to our own lives and service.

The Letter to the Hebrews exhorts us to perseverance and earnestness in renewed faith and hope. Now is not the time to grow careless; now is the time to imitate those who have remained steadfast to the end. These are not simply empty words, a rhetorical exhortation to be of good cheer. The New Testament acknowledges that there will be trials and temptations, that perseverance will not always be easy, that our faith and hope will be tested. But the New Testament also teaches that we can surmount these trials and temptations in Christ Jesus: "No testing has overtaken you that is not common to everyone. God is faithful, and he will not let you be tested beyond your strength, but with the testing he will also provide the way out so that you may be able to endure it" (1 Corinthians 10:13).

In other words, do not be surprised that you are being tempted. Don't give up at the midpoint of your Christian life simply because things are no longer as easy as they once were. And do not spend a lot of time bemoaning your newly discovered weakness. Focus rather on the strength of Jesus Christ, given to you so that you can surmount whatever trial or temptation afflicts you.

In the New Testament's teaching on steadfastness, the focus is not on our own strength and endurance, although those are certainly necessary for us to persevere. Rather, it emphasizes God's role in giving us strength: "It is God who is at work in you, enabling you both to will and to work for his good pleasure" (Philippians 2:13). Therefore, our confidence need not be in ourselves (we know how weak we are), but in God, that he will see us through to the end. "The one who calls you is faithful, and he will do this" (1 Thessalonians 5:24).

At midday, we can both look back upon the time that has gone before and look forward to all that lies ahead. Because of God's love for us, we can look ahead with confidence and hope: "I am confident of this, that the one who began a good work among you will bring it to completion by the day of Jesus Christ" (Philippians 1:6).

3. TAKE COURAGE

> And when [Jesus] got into the boat, his disciples followed him. A windstorm arose on the sea, so great that the boat was being swamped by the waves; but he was asleep. And they went and woke him up, saying, "Lord, save us! We are perishing!" And he said to them, "Why are you afraid, you of little faith?" Then he got up and rebuked the winds and the sea; and there was a dead calm.
>
> —Matthew 8:23-26

Jesus often had to exhort his followers to greater faith and courage in the midst of trying circumstances. It is significant that whenever Jesus told the disciples to "be not afraid," they had good reason to be afraid. Some of his disciples were fishermen and were well acquainted with the hazards of storms on the Sea of Galilee. Their fear during a storm while Jesus slept was a well-informed fear. They were not "landlubbers" panicking at the sight of a few waves; they were professional sailors who realized that they were sinking. Nevertheless, Jesus chided them for being frightened while he was present in the boat.

Jesus' message to the woman who had suffered from a hemorrhage for twelve years was, "Take heart [or have courage], daughter; your faith has made you well" (Matthew 9:22). It took faith and courage on her part to approach Jesus for healing. She had to believe that she could still be healed even after having endured many treatments that had depleted her money without improving her health (Mark 5:26). She needed courage and faith to push her way through a crowd to approach

Jesus, despite suffering from a disease that made her ritually unclean and therefore a social outcast. Jesus' exhortation to have courage was not an idle platitude, but a message that directly addressed her need.

Likewise, when Jesus told his disciples, "Do not let your hearts be troubled" (John 14:1), he was speaking to a specific situation in which the disciples had good reason to have troubled hearts: they were eating a last supper with Jesus on the eve of his death, and they had learned that one of them would betray him and another deny him (13:21, 38). Yet Jesus told them to continue trusting him with untroubled hearts despite what was going to happen.

Today we sometimes find ourselves worried or discouraged, anxious or afraid. It's only human for us to feel fearful when circumstances arise that are beyond our control. When cancer strikes a member of our family, it's only natural for us to fear the worst. When a child turns to drugs and rejects his family's values, it's only natural for his parents to feel helpless. When parents lose their jobs and are unsure how they will support their family and pay their bills, it's only natural for them to feel anxious. If we had been in the boat with the disciples during the storm, we would have been worried too.

Yet in all these situations, Jesus' message to us is, "Be not afraid." He does not say that, humanly speaking, everything is fine: he did not deny that there was a storm at sea. But he does say that we are not to be fearful even in the face of death itself.

Obviously then, our peace cannot be based on having everything turn out as we would like. As in the gospel incidents, our peace must be based on the presence of Jesus in our lives, in his love for us, in his power. Our freedom from fear must be rooted in our faith in Jesus Christ, not in our own ability to handle any problem that might arise.

If we are still victims of fear and anxiety, if we let the circumstances of our lives depress us, it is a sign that our eyes are not firmly enough fixed on Jesus. If we lack an abiding peace, we are not yet fully grounding our lives on God's love for us—a love that neither human failings nor sickness nor death can ever diminish.

4. PRUNING

> [Jesus said:] "I am the true vine, and my Father is the vinegrower. He removes every branch in me that bears no fruit. Every branch that bears fruit he prunes to make it bear more fruit."
>
> —John 15:1-2

In his teaching, Jesus used examples that were familiar to his audience. When he wanted to make a point about the kingdom of God, he would illustrate it by talking about the size of seeds or the problems that farmers faced keeping their fields free of weeds—knowing that seeds and weeds were everyday realities to his followers. And when Jesus wished to teach about an aspect of his Father's love for us, he made his message vivid by talking about raising grapes. Many of his disciples probably had grapevines growing in the courtyards of their houses and had learned from their parents how to care for them. Jesus' words about grapevines had a meaning for them that those of us who buy our grapes at the grocery store might easily miss.

When trials or setbacks come our way, we wonder why. When we are disappointed or discouraged, we wonder whether God still loves us or whether he has forgotten about us. Jesus knew that his followers would face such times. He told them that they would be brought to maturity and fruitfulness in the Christian life through such trials and difficulties, just as a grapevine is made more fruitful through pruning.

A good farmer knows that he needs to prune every vine, no matter how healthy it is, in order for it to bear the best fruit it can. Pruning is a normal part of the life of a healthy grapevine.

One of the purposes of pruning is to control the amount of grapes that a vine will bear: through pruning, a vine will grow fewer, but higher-quality, grapes. If a vine is allowed to grow without pruning, it will bud forth many more clusters of grapes than it has the strength to bring to maturity. Pruning cuts back a vine to produce the largest crop of grapes that it can grow well.

Our Father's pruning action in our lives has a similar function. His pruning is not a sign that he has rejected us or is gravely dissatisfied with us—it is a sign that he wants us to be healthy and to bear good fruit. His pruning action is a normal part of the Christian life, not a mark that we are particularly bad or unfruitful. His pruning is not only for beginning Christians but a continuing necessity for all of us. Sometimes his pruning forces us back to what is most important in our lives and makes us focus once again on bearing good fruit in these high-priority areas.

Sometimes we are tempted to believe that we are not merely being pruned but have become dead wood that is being cut off from the vine. Sometimes we can't see that our lives are bearing much fruit. But there are times and seasons in the Christian life, just as there are times and seasons in the life of a grapevine. Pruning takes place during the time of the year when a vine is dormant and not bearing fruit; pruning is the preparation for next year's crop. In the course of pruning, a vinedresser will remove any dead wood; a good vinedresser can easily tell the difference between a branch that is dead and a branch that is merely dormant. The good vinedresser can see the signs of life beneath the apparently dead exterior, and will prune that branch so that it will bear good fruit next season.

A dead branch has no feeling and does not know that it is being cut from the vine. Perhaps that gives us a way of knowing that we are not dead branches being cut off but living branches being pruned: if it still hurts, we are only being pruned. And that means that the Father sees life in us and is lovingly preparing us for our next season of harvest.

5. THE STRENGTH OF CLAY

For we do not proclaim ourselves; we proclaim Jesus Christ as Lord and ourselves as your slaves for Jesus' sake. For it is the God who said, "Let light shine out of darkness," who has shone in our hearts to give the light of the knowledge of the glory of God in the face of Jesus Christ.

But we have this treasure in clay jars, so that it may be made clear that this extraordinary power belongs to God and does not come from us.

—2 Corinthians 4:5-7

Archaeologists digging up the remains of ancient cities in Palestine inevitably discover great quantities of clay pottery. By tracing the changes through time in the design of jars, pots, and dishes, scholars can reconstruct the rise and fading of societies, the migration of peoples, the destruction of nations.

Clay was a commonly used material in the ancient Near East. Clay could be molded into bricks and dried in the sun, and houses constructed from such bricks. Clay could be formed into jars and dishes and water jugs, and baked in simple furnaces. Clay jars were fragile; if they were dropped, they shattered.

Paul used this fact of everyday life to illustrate one of the paradoxes of the gospel. We have been given a great treasure: life in Jesus Christ. But we carry this treasure in the common clay jar of ourselves. It is as if a wealthy woman kept a supply of the most costly perfume in the world in a rude and cracked clay pot.

We know our unworthiness before God. A clay jar is not worthy to hold precious ointment; alabaster or gold should be used instead. We are merely clay, but the glory of God has been poured into our lives nonetheless. We know our chips and cracks; we know where our lives are out of round. Yet despite our human flaws, the treasure of the Holy Spirit has been given to us. Clearly God loves us not because we have earned his love, but because he is love.

We also know our weakness and fragility. If a clay jar is knocked off a table, it shatters, and its contents spill out onto the dust of the floor. Although God's life has been poured into us, we remain fragile nonetheless. The power that is manifest in our lives comes not from ourselves but from the treasure that we carry inside us. We are not brass jugs, capable of surviving knocks and blows through stoical determination. We are clay jars, dependent upon God's protection for our survival.

We are right to acknowledge the source of our strength; yet we need to be careful not to overemphasize our weakness. The fact that archeologists today discover jars and pots that have survived intact for over 2,000 years is a testimony to the staying power of common clay. Iron rusts, wood rots, but clay often endures. So it is with us. Many of us underestimate our inner resources, our capacity for surviving hardship, our ability to begin ever anew to reshape our lives according to God's call. We are fragile—but not as fragile as a flower. Our endurance is limited—but it is real endurance nonetheless. God's power operates in our weakness—and our weakness is no reason to despair. As Paul wrote, "He said to me, 'My grace is sufficient for you, for power is made perfect in weakness.' So I will boast all the more gladly of my weaknesses, so that the power of Christ may dwell in me" (2 Corinthians 12:9).

As clay receptacles of the love of God, we, like Paul, "are afflicted in every way, but not crushed; perplexed, but not driven to despair; persecuted, but not forsaken; struck down, but not destroyed; always carrying in the body the death of Jesus, so that the life of Jesus may also be made visible in our bodies" (2 Corinthians 4:8-10).

6. CASE STUDY: THE ISRAELITES IN EXILE

For I, the LORD your God,
    hold your right hand;
it is I who say to you, "Do not fear,
    I will help you."
Do not fear, you worm Jacob,
    you insect Israel!
I will help you, says the LORD;
    your Redeemer is the Holy One of Israel.
—Isaiah 41:13-14

These words of consolation were addressed to Israelites living in exile in Babylon after the Babylonian army had conquered and destroyed Jerusalem and exiled many of its inhabitants. If the Israelites ever needed a message of hope and consolation, it was during this period when God seemed to have abandoned them.

God promised Abraham that he would give the land of

Canaan to his descendants. God spoke to Moses from the burning bush and promised to bring his people "to a good and broad land, a land flowing with milk and honey, to the country of the Canaanites" (Exodus 3:8). God renewed his promise on Mount Sinai and repeatedly reminded his people of it afterward.

Within the promised land, Jerusalem occupied a place of prominence. After David conquered it, he made it his capital and moved the Ark of the Covenant there. Solomon built the great Temple in Jerusalem, which became the center of worship for God's people.

Then hard times came. Division splintered the nation into a northern kingdom and a southern kingdom. The divided kingdoms were not able to preserve the political independence that the people had under David, nor was either kingdom ever able to recapture the splendor of Solomon's reign.

The northern kingdom fell to the armies of Assyria in 721 B.C., and massive deportations took place. Jerusalem and the southern kingdom maintained a precarious existence until 586, when Jerusalem was destroyed by Babylon and its citizens carried off into exile. The kingdom of David was no more; the temple built by Solomon was reduced to rubble.

Had God abandoned his people? Had he taken back his promises? Had he forgotten his covenant? How could he allow his people to be so thoroughly devastated, to be left in such a pitiful state?

God had not abandoned his people; he was still faithful to his covenant. In very little time, Cyrus the Persian would conquer Babylon and allow the exiles to return home to Jerusalem. The temple would be rebuilt; once more Zion would be filled with psalms.

Israelites living in exile had difficulty foreseeing this rescue. The destruction of Jerusalem and their exile from it made

no sense to them. God seemed to have gone back on his promises, even allowing his special dwelling place of the temple to
be destroyed.

Then God spoke to the exiles through a prophet to reassure
them: "I am holding you by your right hand; do not fear." Even
though you are weak and puny compared to the Babylonian
empire, do not focus on your weakness, you "worm Jacob,
you insect Israel." Pay attention instead to him who helps you:
"your Redeemer [rescuer] is the Holy One of Israel." He has a
plan for you that surpasses your hopes and vision.

While few of us are so sorely afflicted as the Israelites
during their time of exile, we are put to the test nonetheless.
Things often do not go according to our plans or expectations.
Divisions separate one Christian from another. The works of
God that we so eagerly dedicate ourselves to are sometimes
dashed to the ground, like the Temple of Jerusalem. We have
a hard time understanding God's plan from the midst of our
disappointment and pain, and we are tempted to lose hope.
The appearance of our lives seems to gainsay the promises we
have received from God.

God's word to us is the same as his word to the Israelites
in exile: "I have chosen you and not cast you off; do not
fear, for I am with you; do not be afraid, for I am your God"
(Isaiah 41:9-10). Even if we feel as lowly as a worm or an
insect, we can depend on God to take us by the hand and
raise us up.

QUESTIONS FOR REFLECTION

1. Have you ever been tempted to turn back from following
   Jesus? What was the root of the temptation? How did
   God's grace strengthen you and enable you to persevere?

2. Have you ever felt like you were in the storm-tossed boat with the disciples, and that Jesus seemed oblivious to what you were going through? What worries or anxieties are weighing you down now? Are you able to hear Jesus saying to you, "Be not afraid"?

3. How have you experienced God's pruning action in your life, cutting away what needed to be trimmed so that you can be healthy and bear good fruit? What was the outcome of his pruning?

4. Isaiah uses the images of a worm and an insect for the Israelites; Paul uses the image of a clay jar for followers of Christ. What mental image do you have of yourself in relation to God? What does this image tell you about your relationship with God?

PART NINE

LIVING FOR THE FUTURE

1. LET EARTH REJOICE

O sing to the LORD a new song;
    sing to the LORD, all the earth.
Sing to the LORD, bless his name;
    tell of his salvation from day to day.
Declare his glory among the nations,
    his marvelous works among all the peoples.
For great is the LORD, and greatly
       to be praised;
    he is to be revered above all gods.
For all the gods of the peoples are idols,
    but the LORD made the heavens. . . .
Let the heavens be glad, and let
       the earth rejoice;
    let the sea roar, and all that fills it;
    let the field exult, and everything in it.
Then shall all the trees of the forest
       sing for joy.

—Psalm 96:1-5, 11-12

Psalm 96 is a psalm of near ecstatic praise; we cannot imagine anyone truly grasping its meaning and yet praying it calmly. For indeed, "great is the LORD and greatly to be praised." He is to be praised not only by those who specialize in praise (monks, for instance) but by all the earth. The heavens and the earth, the sea and the fields, even trees are to join in the new song of praise for God. The people of every nation are to praise God, recognizing that he alone is God, the Creator of the universe, and that his power and majesty call for a response of praise.

Psalm 96 presents a compelling case for praising God; it is a psalm that we can throw ourselves into during our times of prayer. But it is also a psalm that calls for something that we don't experience much today. We live in a world in which millions of people don't acknowledge God. When we leave the chapel or room in which we pray and go back out into the world, we find that it is not a world of praise of God. In fact, the human race largely seems to get along without recognizing any need to praise God. Hence we may feel a contrast between our prayer and the rest of our lives: we pray in the belief that we worship the Creator and Redeemer of the universe, yet we live and work in situations that acknowledge little dependence on God.

Our problem is the opposite of the difficulty the psalmist faced. In his time there was a superabundance of gods competing for allegiance; every nation had its gods, every land, its idols. Israelites had to resist the temptation to worship these false gods. Psalm 96 upholds the unique position of God: "He is to be revered above all gods. For all the gods of the peoples are idols" (verses 4-5).

In our time, however, we are tempted by atheism rather than polytheism. We are tempted to believe that the world can get along with no God at all rather than tempted to believe in too many gods. Instead of living in a world in which the sun and the moon are worshiped as gods, we live in a world where many do not acknowledge the Creator of the sun and the moon and the rest of the universe.

Belief is not completely absent from the world; rather, it has been compartmentalized and largely restricted to churches. God is privately worshiped but publicly ignored. Belief in God has become a matter of personal opinion and preference, rather than being the public faith of a nation and the basis of a common life of a people. Perhaps this is inevitable given the increasingly cosmopolitan nature of modern societies and the need for nations to respect the beliefs—or lack of beliefs—of all their citizens.

We must pray Psalm 96 as a prayer of hope, a prayer looking forward to the time when all creation will join in praise of God. Psalm 96 exhorts us to hasten this day by our own witness and work: "Declare his glory among the nations, his marvelous works among all peoples" (verse 3). Psalm 96 promises that the day of the Lord will come: "He is coming to judge the earth. He will judge the world with righteousness and the peoples with his truth" (verse 13). To this we may add the prayer with which the Bible ends: "Amen. Come, Lord Jesus!" (Revelation 22:20-21).

2. THE SPIRIT IN THE CHURCH

Then certain individuals came down from Judea and were teaching the brothers, "Unless you are circumcised according to the custom of Moses, you cannot be saved." And after Paul and Barnabas had no small dissension and debate with them, Paul and Barnabas and some of the others were appointed to go up to Jerusalem to discuss this question with the apostles and the elders.

—Acts 15:1-2

The church on Pentecost day was a Jewish church, made up of the followers that Jesus had left behind in Jerusalem when he ascended into heaven. After Pentecost the gospel quickly spread beyond Judea to cities like Antioch, and soon many gentiles began to believe in the good news about Jesus Christ. This raised questions: Did non-Jewish converts to Christianity also have to become converts to Judaism? Were they to be bound by the Law of Moses?

The explicit teachings of Jesus while he was on earth did not resolve these questions; he had conducted his public ministry mainly among Jews. Hence, unanswered questions faced the early church, brought to a head by the missionary activities of Paul.

In retrospect, this state of affairs is surprising. Surely Jesus should have realized that gentiles would join his Jewish disciples in the early church and that this would raise the question of whether gentile converts were to follow the Law of Moses, accepting circumcision if they were men. Surely Jesus could have resolved the question with a few simple, direct words. But the evidence of the New Testament is that he did not. So we are left to wonder, why didn't he?

Although Jesus didn't leave behind explicit instructions that would have prevented the first serious crisis in the church, he did provide the means for resolving this and all future crises the church would face. He left behind a group of leaders to whom he had given authority, and he sent his Holy Spirit upon them to guide them as they guided the church.

After Paul and Barnabas reached Jerusalem, there was a prolonged discussion over the question of gentile converts. "After there had been much debate" (Acts 15:7), Peter intervened, siding with Paul (15:7-11). James, the presiding elder of the Jerusalem church, concurred with Peter (15:19-21). A letter was drafted that conveyed the decision to those who had sent Paul and Barnabas to Jerusalem. The letter stated, "It has seemed good to the Holy Spirit and to us" that gentile converts are not bound by all the prescriptions of the Mosaic law (15:28-29).

The matter was resolved not by the explicit teachings of Jesus but by the Holy Spirit working through those responsible for guiding the church. Jesus left behind a body of basic teachings, valid for all time, but he realized that he could not address the innumerable questions that would face the church throughout the ages. Jesus did not attempt to resolve them himself. Instead he left behind his authority and his Spirit, operating in those responsible for leading the church.

The plan adopted by Jesus should be a source of confidence for us. Not only have we received the teachings of Jesus from his years on earth, but we have the presence of the Holy Spirit, working through those who have been given the mission of guiding the church. We can have confidence in the word of God that we read in Scripture. And we can also have confidence that this word is heard and applied today by those in authority over the church. We can have the same confidence that the Christian communities in Antioch and Syria and Cilicia (Acts 15:23) had when they received the letter from Jerusalem. The Holy Spirit had spoken through Peter and James, and we can be confident that the same Holy Spirit guides the church today.

3. ALIVE IN CHRIST

Do you not know that all of us who have been baptized into Christ Jesus were baptized into his death? Therefore we have been buried with him by baptism into death, so that, just as Christ was raised from the dead by the glory of the Father, we too might walk in newness of life.

For if we have been united with him in a death like his, we will certainly be united with him in a resurrection like his. We know that our old self was crucified with him so that the body of sin might be destroyed, and we might no longer be enslaved to sin. For whoever has died is freed from sin. . . . So you also must consider yourselves dead to sin and alive to God in Christ Jesus.

—Romans 6:3-7, 11

Paul's words about what happens to us in baptism are revolutionary words. They speak of death and new life. They speak of our being transformed in Jesus by a change more profound than the transformation of matter into energy in a nuclear reactor. Yet they are perhaps over-familiar words to us now, words that have lost their revolutionary impact on our lives.

As an exercise to help bring Paul's teaching to life for us again, imagine that one day you wake up not feeling very well. You think that it is probably the flu and that a few days in bed will take care of it. But after your sickness lingers on for a week, you go to see your family doctor. He examines you more carefully than you thought he would, and then he quietly tells you that he wants you to be examined by another doctor, a specialist. With some fear now, you see the other doctor, who performs all sorts of tests and tells you to come back in a week, when the results are in.

It is a week of considerable anxiety for you. You have been pretty healthy all your life. You are wrapped up in your family and your work; you have too many irons in the fire to be sick just now. You wonder what disease you might have.

When you go back to the specialist, he informs you that you are suffering from a rare, fatal disease, for which there is no known cure. When you ask him how long you have to live, he tells you that he can't be certain but that it is probably only a matter of weeks.

How would you live out the remaining weeks of your life? What would you think was most important to do, now that you had so little time left? What things did you previously think were important that would now seem trivial in comparison? Who would you give your possessions to? Who would you express your love to? What would you repent of and seek forgiveness for? Who would you forgive? How would you make use of each moment, now that so few remained? How would you spend time with God in prayer?

Suppose further, however, that as you lay in bed some weeks later, resigned to death, your strength rapidly ebbing, the specialist came in to see you and said that there was an experimental drug he could give you that would not cure you, but might delay your death and allow you to live a normal life in the meantime. Its drawback was that when death came, it would come suddenly, without warning, and that there was no way of knowing whether this would happen in a day, a week, or a year. You agree to take the drug, and find that it does indeed remove the symptoms of your illness, enabling you to live a normal life once again. But for how long, you don't know.

Now how would you live, as one brought back from the dead? What would your prayer of thanksgiving be for the gift of life? How would you carry through on all the decisions you had made before, when you thought you were at death's door? How would you live, knowing how uncertain the length of your new life would be?

The reality of our death in baptism and new life in Jesus is much more profound than a reprieve from physical death. It should have an even more profound impact on our lives than an experience of imminent death and an unexpected rescue. The words of Paul call for radically transformed lives: "So you also must consider yourselves dead to sin and alive to God in Christ Jesus."

4. THE FUTURE

> Then Isaiah said to Hezekiah, "Hear the word of the Lord: Days are coming when all that is in your house, and that which your ancestors have stored up until this day, shall be carried to Babylon; nothing shall be left, says the Lord. Some of your own sons who are born

to you shall be taken away; they shall be eunuchs in the palace of the king of Babylon." Then Hezekiah said to Isaiah, "The word of the LORD that you have spoken is good." For he thought, "Why not, if there will be peace and security in my days?"

—2 Kings 20:16-19

Hezekiah ruled over Judah during the time of Isaiah and the destruction of Samaria by Assyria. His 29-year reign interrupted an otherwise dreary succession of faithless kings who led God's people into the worship of false gods.

Hezekiah "did what was right in the sight of the LORD," abolishing pagan shrines and idols. "He trusted in the LORD God of Israel; so that there was no one like him among all the kings of Judah after him, or among those who were before him. For he held fast to the LORD; he did not depart from following him but kept the commandments that the LORD commanded Moses. The LORD was with him; wherever he went, he prospered" (2 Kings 18:3-7). God once healed Hezekiah when he was at the point of death, confirming his healing with a sign (20:1-11).

But even though Hezekiah was a very good king, he was not without his lapses. He welcomed visitors from Babylon to Jerusalem, probably seeking to form an alliance with them against Assyria. To impress them he showed them all the wealth in his treasury and storehouses (2 Kings 20:12-15). When Isaiah heard about it, he delivered the prophecy to Hezekiah that foretold that this wealth would be carried off to Babylon.

It was foolish for Hezekiah to think of an alliance with Babylon: God could protect Jerusalem against Assyria without Babylonian help. And it was folly to show the Babylonians Jerusalem's wealth, for they might covet it. In fact, it would be Babylon and not Assyria that would conquer Jeru-

149

salem and haul away its treasures, enslaving the descendants of Hezekiah.

But Hezekiah took Isaiah's prophetic reprimand as good news: It meant that Jerusalem was safe during his lifetime. He did not seem to care what happened to his children or his people after he died; he was seemingly content to have disaster come, as long as it came tomorrow.

How could such a good man as Hezekiah fall into such shortsighted selfishness? We do not know. But the fact that someone so devoted to God and so pleasing to God could fall into such a callous attitude can serve as a warning to us not to make the same mistake.

And we often find ourselves tempted to make just such a mistake. The world and its problems are so complex that we find it easier not to think about them. Are our energy resources being depleted at a rate that will exhaust them during our children's or grandchildren's lifetimes? We don't worry about it very much as long as there is still enough gasoline to power our cars today. Does the worldwide imbalance between the rich and the poor, the haves and the have-nots, create a permanently unstable political situation? We can try to ignore it as long as our lives are relatively untouched by wars or revolutions. Are there environmental issues that might become critical in the decades ahead? They are secondary concerns, as long as they don't threaten us now. The complexity of these problems and their lack of immediate impact on us allow us to ignore them—but our children and grandchildren will inherit what we bequeath to them.

We should perhaps feel sympathy for Hezekiah: it was not easy to be king of Judah in the face of an almost constant threat from Assyrian military might. It was probably easy for him to be grateful for peace today and ignore what might come tomorrow. And given the challenges we face, it would be easy for us to fall into the same shortsightedness. Rather, we need to broaden our vision and do whatever we can to solve the world's worsening problems, lest we leave them to our children as a bitter inheritance.

5. OUR HOPE IN CHRIST

If Christ has not been raised, then our proclamation has been in vain and your faith has been in vain. We are even found to be misrepresenting God, because we testified of God that he raised Christ—whom he did not raise if it is true that the dead are not raised. For if the dead are not raised, then Christ has not been raised. If Christ has not been raised, your faith is futile and you are still in your sins. Then those also who have died in Christ have perished. If for this life only we have hoped in Christ, we are of all people most to be pitied.

—1 Corinthians 15:14-19

The gospel is a message of hope for us. Christ has died, Christ is risen, Christ will come again. We have participated in his death through baptism; we hope to participate in his resurrection to eternal life.

But the gospel also makes some difficult demands of us. Many of the teachings of Jesus run counter to the values of this world; some even seem to defy logic and experience. We can be tempted to skip over these teachings without taking them too seriously, thinking, "Jesus couldn't possibly have meant that." But if we are to hear the word of God clearly, we must be willing to confront the full meaning of these statements and face up to their full implications for our lives.

The beatitudes in the gospels of Matthew and Luke reverse our normal values. "Blessed are you who are poor, for yours is the kingdom of God. Blessed are you who are hungry now, for you will be filled" (Luke 6:20-21). We naturally view poverty and hunger as undesirable, as conditions to be eradicated. It is hard for us to see how anyone who is poor or hungry could be considered blessed.

On the other hand, the success that the world strives for is decried by Jesus: "Woe to you who are rich, for you have received your consolation. Woe to you who are full now, for you will be hungry" (Luke 6:24-25). We are not quite sure what to make of Jesus' words or what to do about them.

There are other teachings of Jesus that are equally discomforting: "Do not resist an evildoer. . . . Give to everyone who begs from you. . . . Love your enemies" (Matthew 5:39, 42, 44). "If any want to become my followers, let them deny themselves and take up their cross and follow me" (Mark 8:34). Jesus seems to make unreasonable demands upon us, demands that go beyond common sense.

It is this streak of unreasonableness in the gospel that Paul might have had in mind when he wrote, "If for this life only we have hoped in Christ, we are of all people most to be pitied" (1 Corinthians 15:19). If we do attempt to conform our lives to the gospel, then we may have to give up things that are part of a good and decent human life. If we stake our lives on the hope of rising in Christ, then we must live as people who have such a hope—and that means living quite differently than we would if we did not have that hope.

The call of Christ is not merely a call to live a decent and reasonably generous life. Many who do not believe in Christ live such lives, following their conscience and sense of justice. We should respect them as upright and honorable people.

Our call is to do something more: we are called to imitate Christ, even to the point of laying down our lives. We are called to obey him, even when what he asks of us goes beyond what is reasonable according to this world's standards. We are called to live as if we really believe we are destined to rise to eternal life. And we are called to risk everything on the basis of that belief.

The gospel is not merely a collection of lofty ideals and difficult demands. The gospel is first of all good news: that God the Father loves us, that we are offered the life of the Spirit through Jesus Christ, and that resurrection awaits us. But the gospel also makes demands of us, and not everything that Jesus asks of us is easy.

In fact, if we do find the call of Jesus to be easy, then we may need to examine whether we are truly hearing all that Jesus asks of us. If we feel completely at home in this world, then it makes no sense for Paul to claim that we are the most pitiable of people. Our hope in Christ is not for this world only, or for merely a pleasant life in this world. Our hope in Christ is for eternity.

6. THE PERSPECTIVE OF ETERNITY

> [Jesus said:] "This is indeed the will of my Father, that all who see the Son and believe in him may have eternal life; and I will raise them up on the last day."
>
> —John 6:40

Jesus' promise of eternal life transforms the meaning of our life on earth. His promise also challenges our values, and demands that we change our perspective of what is important and what is unimportant.

From a medical standpoint, life ends with death. Death comes as a tragic separation between lover and beloved, between child and parent, between lifelong friends. Death disrupts the highest human happiness we can experience, the love of two persons for each other.

Sometimes death comes out of season, taking away a young person barely setting out on life. Sometimes death takes away someone we were counting on to help us: a political leader who could arouse hope, a scientist working on a cure for cancer, a writer able to inspire us. And sometimes death seems to come sadly late, after an elderly person has suffered the ravages of Alzheimer's disease for many years.

If our earthly life is but a prelude to an eternity with Christ, however, our perspective is radically changed. Then there is no permanent separation between those united in love. Then there is really no such thing as a death too early or a death too late. Then we need not lose hope for those whose last years are a sad decline: they shall once again be the persons they were and more. They shall experience a resurrection of their bodies that frees them from the accumulated disabilities of decades; they shall once again rejoice in the fullness of life.

The perspective of eternity transforms our view of all who seem to have been shortchanged by life. Those born severely mentally disabled might seem incomplete persons unless we can anticipate their completion in eternity. Those who are victims of incapacitating disabilities and birth defects, consigned to a life of dependence, might seem to us to have been cruelly robbed of life, unless we know in faith that their disabilities will be repaired a thousand times over in eternity.

The perspective of eternity must also shape our view of the unborn. If no spark of human life will ever die out, then the life of the unborn must be reverenced as much as the life of the born. If God can raise up with new bodies those whose earthly bodies are deformed and ravaged, then he can give resurrected bodies even to those whose earthly bodies never had a chance to develop fully.

The prospect of eternal life must also change our evaluation of those whose earthly life is one of poverty and suffering.

We can have the hope that those whose present life is one of misery will find rest and reward in the next life. But even more, our prospect of sharing eternal life with them highlights our obligation to them here and now. I cannot turn my back on the starvation of refugees on the other side of the world; I shall be with them in eternity, and I have an obligation to them now. I cannot ignore the suffering of anyone who may be my room-mate in heaven, so to speak; I cannot harden my heart toward any other human being.

There will be a judgment for each of us as we enter eternal life. We must live in hope of passing that judgment through the redemption that Jesus Christ has given us. We must also hold that hope for others, that they too will be saved through the mystery of God's love for them. Our expectation can be that we will be able to love for all eternity those we love now on earth. Our hope can be that those who do not experience the fullness of life on this earth will experience it in the presence of their Father in heaven. Our obligation must be to reverence everyone as intended for resurrection into eternal life with us.

7. THE FINAL EXAM

One of the criminals who were hanged there kept deriding him and saying, "Are you not the Messiah? Save yourself and us!" But the other rebuked him, saying, "Do you not fear God, since you are under the same sentence of condemnation? And we indeed have been condemned justly, for we are getting what we deserve for our deeds, but this man has done nothing wrong." Then he said, "Jesus, remember me when you come into your kingdom." He replied, "Truly I tell you, today you will be with me in Paradise."

—Luke 23:39-43

There were once two teachers on a school faculty. The first teacher didn't enjoy teaching and didn't really like students. He made no effort to make his lectures interesting, yet he punished any students who didn't pay attention. Before school let out each year, he would administer a very long and difficult final exam. It was designed to uncover everything the students hadn't learned, and he graded it very strictly. Students lived in dread all year of the exam they would face at the end.

The second teacher genuinely loved students and worked very hard to help them learn. Her greatest joy came when a student grasped a new idea or succeeded in learning a new skill. She spent extra time with those who had the hardest time learning. She liked to be around students and sometimes invited them over to her house for dinner. She also gave a final exam each year, but she designed it to find out what her students had learned, not what they hadn't learned. There were no trick questions, and her students knew that she was rooting for them to pass it.

If we were to imagine God to be a teacher, we might have a tendency to think that he would be like the first kind of teacher. We might imagine that God tolerates us but doesn't really find any enjoyment in us. Life in the cosmic classroom of this teacher would be bound by many rules, and we could expect sure punishment if we disobeyed any of them. We would be very unsure that we would pass the final judgment of this teacher, and we would live our lives in quiet dread of the day we would have to face it.

Jesus came to teach us about God, and he did it by being a faithful mirror of his Father. The God that Jesus revealed by his life was not like the first teacher but the second.

Jesus found delight in being with us: "Zacchaeus, hurry and come down; for I must stay at your house today" (Luke 19:5). He did not hold himself aloof from sinners but sought them out to help them. "Those who are well have no need of a physician, but those who are sick" (Luke 5:31). Jesus' goal was not to catch people in their sin but to deliver them from sin. "Has no one condemned you?" Jesus asked the woman who was caught in the act of adultery. "Neither do I condemn you. Go your way, and from now on do not sin again" (John 8:10-11). Just as the second teacher found joy in seeing her students learn, so Jesus found joy in seeing his disciples come to know God: "Jesus rejoiced in the Holy Spirit and said, 'I thank you, Father, Lord of heaven and earth, because you have hidden these things from the wise and the intelligent and revealed them to infants'" (Luke 10:21).

Jesus also taught us that the last judgment will be like the final exam of the second teacher. There will be no trick questions. God will not be aiming at finding enough fault in us to condemn us but enough faithfulness to reward us. If God were trying to find a way to "fail" us, he would never have sent Jesus into the world to die for us.

The thieves who were crucified with Jesus had led lives of crime. One of them, however, admitted that his punishment was deserved and asked Jesus to remember him in his kingdom. His request was a very simple act of faith, but Jesus' response was immediate and unconditional: "Truly I tell you, today you will be with me in Paradise" (Luke 23:43). No one else in the gospel accounts receives such firm assurance of salvation from Jesus. And by our standards, no one deserved it less! But Jesus did not focus on the life of crime that this man had led; Jesus only focused on his few simple words of faith. It was as if a teacher knew that a student had only learned one thing all year, and therefore asked only that question on the final exam.

"Indeed, God did not send the Son into the world to condemn the world, but in order that the world might be saved through him" (John 3:17).

QUESTIONS FOR REFLECTION

1. What support do you find in the church for living out your faith in a world that does not share your faith? How does a conviction that the Holy Spirit guides the church help you weather whatever storms may buffet the church?

2. How does your union with Christ give a sense of newness and adventure to your life? Are you able to live each day as if it were your last day on earth? Are you able to strive each day as if the consequences of what you do will have an effect on future generations?

3. Would your values and practices make sense if you had no hope of resurrection? How does the prospect of living with God forever affect how you live right now? How does the hope of enjoying eternal life with others shape how you relate to them now?

4. Do you look forward to the last judgment with dread because of your sins or with confidence because of God's love for you? What hope do you find in Jesus' words to the "good thief"? What would you like your last prayer to be before you face God's final exam?

Other Books of Interest:

The Catholic Book of Scripture Passages
A Prayer Guide for Every Occasion
Compiled by Lucy Scholand

Scripture speaks to our hearts—and to our every need. In this compilation, Catholics can find just the right Scripture passage to pray at just the right moment. This book will be a constant companion for those seeking the Lord before and after Mass, Communion, and the Sacrament of Reconciliation, as well as the other sacraments. Suggested Scripture passages for healing and for freedom from fear, worry, and depression, are also offered. Other sections include verses to pray morning and night; verses to honor Mary and the saints; and passages for the liturgical seasons.
176 pages, 4½ x 6¼, softcover, $9.95
Item# BPRYE5

The Story of the Bible
How It Came to Us
Henry Wansbrough, OSB

The Bible has a story behind it. How did it come to us in its current form? Why did a number of early gospels never make it into the canon of Scripture? Which is the authentic text of the Bible? How was the Bible translated into English? A leading international Scripture scholar, Fr. Henry Wansbrough, OSB, provides the answers to these questions and many more in this balanced, fast-paced, and entertaining account.
5⅜" x 8½," softcover, 140 pages, $11.95
Item# BBIBE6